SCHOLASTIC

Just-Right Comprehension Mini-Lessons

GRADE 1

21, 22, 23, 36, 38,
41, 69, 75, 76, 83
111, 113

CHERYL M. SIGMON

New York • Toronto • London • Auckland • Sydney
Mexico City • New Delhi • Hong Kong • Buenos Aires

Teaching Resources

Dedication

To Merryl Maleska Wilbur—You've done it again—made my ideas clearer and easier for teachers, and you've accomplished it with such polish, sensitivity, and ingenuity. Many thanks for your contributions—numerous and invaluable!

To first-grade teachers who work their magic in wonderful ways during their students' first year of school. I hope this makes your tough but rewarding job easier and that it helps your students to see text in new and different ways.

And, as always, to my husband and best friend in the world, Ray. Thank you for being there for me!

—CMS

Acknowledgements

Rhonda Reed, First-grade teacher, North Miami Elementary School, North Miami, IN

Lisa D. Gilpin, Teacher and consultant, Versailles, IN

Marian S. Hodge, Consultant, Savannah, GA

Sylvia M. Ford, Consultant, Columbia, SC

Administrators and teachers of Sand Creek Elementary School, North Vernon, IN

Dr. Linda Walker, and the teachers and administrators of Montpelier Elementary, Northside Elementary, and Southside Elementary in the Blackford County School District, Hartford City, IN

Peggy Jones, Director, and the teachers and administrators of the Muskogee School District, Muskogee, OK

Linda Gillespie and Deborah Green-Wilson, Title One Office, and the teachers and administrators of Richland School District One, Columbia, SC

Sierra Jackson, Principal, and the teachers of Custer Hill Elementary School, Ft. Riley, KS

Lana Evans, Curriculum Director; Principals Gloria Quattrone, Nancy Thompson, Gilberto Rito, Travis Wilson, Shawna Evans, and Laura Cano and the teachers of Southlawn, Lincoln, Washington, Garfield, MacArthur, and McKinley Elementary Schools of Liberal, KS

Lisa Wiedmann and the teachers of the Rhinelander School System, Rhinelander, WI

Cover design and cover photo by Maria Lilja.
Interior design by Holly Grundon.
Interior photos courtesy of the author.

ISBN-13: 978-0-439-87025-2
ISBN-10: 0-439-87025-9

Printed in the U.S.A.

1 2 3 4 5 6 7 8 9 10 40 15 14 13 12 11 10 09 08 07

Table of Contents

Introduction

Section Three: Generating and Answering Questions

Section Four: Using Graphic and Semantic Organizers

Section Five: Creating and Using Images

Section Six: Accessing Prior Knowledge

Section Seven: Summarizing

Section Eight: Using Text Features and Organizers

Introduction

The focus of this book, reading comprehension, has for several decades been considered the "essence of reading" (Durkin, 1993). Many of us have sat alongside a child who can, with great precision, "call" all the words on a page correctly. However, this same child is clearly lost when asked to talk about the content he or she has just read. Not only do we now know that good word callers are not necessarily really reading but we have changed our instruction accordingly. Over the past recent decades, reading instruction has had at its center the goal of helping students develop good habits—constructing meaning and reading with genuine fluency. In line with that goal, this book aims to help teachers put solid research into practice through simple but powerful daily mini-lessons. The hope is that these mini-lessons can offer students tools and ways of approaching text that turn into lifelong lessons to be applied far beyond the classroom.

Contexts and Frameworks for These Mini-Lessons

These mini-lessons are the teacher's opportunity to provide direct instruction in key comprehension skills and strategies that first graders need to become good readers. The lessons' great advantage is that they can be implemented in a number of different natural classroom contexts. For example, these mini-lessons will work well within guided reading lessons; reading workshops;

tutorial sessions; small-group instruction; and content area lessons, in which understanding about how to read and manage text is important. Here's a brief description of how they might work within each of these contexts:

- **Guided Reading Lessons** The first segment of a guided reading lesson—the time dedicated to a teacher's modeling what students are expected to do during their own reading—is an ideal instructional home for these mini-lessons. Frequently there is also a step in the mini-lesson outline that describes students' own reading and sometimes one that involves the teacher's closure and summarizing. Thus, in several different ways, you should be able to fold these lessons right into the framework of a guided reading lesson.

- **Reading Workshops** The Reading Workshop begins with a teacher's modeling and demonstrating what a good reader does. These mini-lessons are an ideal launch point for the Workshop because direct instruction and modeling lie at the core of the lessons.

- **Tutorial Sessions** These lessons are ideal for use in tutorial sessions that target specific students' needs. Just use the book's table of contents and the Matrix of Standards to locate a lesson that focuses on a particular skill or strategy needed by a student. Also, because the mini-lessons are written step-by-step in a clearly delineated standard format, they should be accessible to all, including assistants supporting regular classroom teachers.

- **Small-Group Instruction** Just as with Tutorial Sessions, these mini-lessons can drastically cut planning time for teachers who need to design lessons for targeted small-group instruction. Identify the common instructional needs of several students and then use the table of contents and the Matrix of Standards to locate the appropriate lesson(s) to teach that skill or strategy.

- **Content Area Lessons** Many of these mini-lessons make use of science or social studies text, thus demonstrating how easy it is to integrate literacy and content instruction. Students need to see how they can use literacy skills to help them make sense of content area information and communicate it to others.

How These Mini-Lessons Were Developed

The curriculum for the lessons in this book is based on a number of documents. As a first step in developing the lessons, I looked into whether educators around the United States generally hold common beliefs about what students need to know and do in first-grade reading comprehension. I selected eleven states that represent different geographical regions as well as diverse populations and studied the standards documents for these states. Not surprisingly, I found a high correlation of commonalities among the documents. Some terminology differed, but the basic thinking was similar. Across the country, it seems that we have pretty much agreed about what constitutes good reading among our first graders.

Next, I studied another important and widely regarded document, *The National Reading Panel Report* (2000), to find out how its experts regard reading comprehension and whether its beliefs are congruent with the states' beliefs. I discovered that while the standards/objectives defined by the states were more discrete and specific than the broader strategies identified in the national document, the two sources corroborated each other and were highly compatible.

Indeed, the two sources work hand-in-hand extremely well. The states' standards can be seen as the focused guidelines necessary to help students achieve the broader, more general strategies suggested by the National Reading Panel. Therefore, in organizing this book and developing the lessons, I used the national strategies as the basis for the section divisions and the more discrete standards as the springboards for the lessons themselves.

Standards

Along with the National Standards, the standards of the following 11 states were gathered to create the curriculum for this book: California, Colorado, Florida, Indiana, Missouri, New York, Pennsylvania, South Carolina, Texas, Virginia, and Washington.

THE NATURE OF A GOOD MINI-LESSON

An effective reading comprehension mini-lesson is direct and explicit and focused solely on the targeted comprehension skill or strategy. Lessons shouldn't confuse the students by introducing grammar, mechanics, usage, long and short vowel sounds, digraphs, and similar skills. There are other opportunities in the instructional day when these skills can best be taught and understood. Reserve your mini-lesson exclusively for those skills and strategies that have direct impact on the meaning derived from reading text.

A teacher's modeling good reading behaviors and thought processes during reading is a critical element of an effective mini-lesson.

There is another key aspect to the effective mini-lesson: While direct and explicit, mini-lesson instruction does not simply tell students what they need to know. Instead, it involves a teacher's active, dynamic modeling of the targeted skill and/or strategy. Modeling the thinking and the decisions that a reader must make, even the little ones, will allow these same thought processes to become part of your students' habits. Thus, a critical part of your modeling is "thinking aloud," or expressing aloud the process you are following as you read a piece of text and apply a strategy or utilize a skill. Many students, especially beginning readers, don't know how to actively reflect as they read. Your demonstrating how to do this becomes a key part of your students' development as readers.

Peeking in on Two Teachers

Here are two mini-lessons that show a clear difference in their approach to instruction. Let's peek into the classrooms below to compare the effectiveness of the two different lessons.

Teacher A

In her classroom, Teacher A gathers students together on the carpet near her rocking chair where she has placed an easel that holds a Big Book. She introduces the book through a quick picture walk to familiarize students with the contents. She then introduces some vocabulary that corresponds to illustrations and teaches the meaning of several related words not in the text. Next she explains to students how to identify the main character in a narrative text. Finally, she invites the students to read along with her as she reads the text. The students seem to enjoy the story. Teacher A concludes the lesson by asking a number of comprehension questions about the story, such as: "Who was the main character?"; "Where did the story take place?"; and "What did Harry say after the dog ran away?"

Teacher B

In his classroom, Teacher B begins a lesson by showing students a handful of seashells he brought back from his summer vacation and asking if any students have ever found shells on a trip to the beach. Then, he shows students the cover of the book the class will read today. He tells them the purpose of today's lesson—making predictions about a book based on the title, cover picture clues, and any other cover information. He explains that he is going to demonstrate the process he goes through himself when he picks up a new book and is not sure what it is about. He tells students, "When I read a book's title and see the pictures on the cover, my brain starts to tell me right away what the book might be about." He offers several ideas aloud, jots down these thoughts on a chart, and then invites students to suggest additional predictions. "Now, we'll read this book and find out if our predictions are right. If they're not, that's okay. We just have to remember to think this way when we read." The teacher reads the story aloud and then holds a brief discussion so that the class can talk about the initial predictions.

At the closure of a well-constructed lesson, you'll likely find students better prepared to answer a most important question. Read on to find out exactly what the question is.

Did the Lesson Succeed?

A great aid to teachers in analyzing the success of reading lessons is asking the simple question: *What did my students learn today that will make them better readers?* And you can make this question even more powerful by asking it directly of students themselves. You may be surprised to hear what your students have to say! Often when we think we're communicating something, it's heard in an entirely different way—especially in dealing with first graders.

This teacher is involving her students actively in their own learning—one hallmark of a good lesson.

If, in answer to this question, students begin to retell the story, they have probably not grown much as readers from the lesson. The students in Teacher A's classroom would be more likely to retell the story. The lesson has several basic shortcomings: It doesn't give students a real reason to care about or even grasp the main purpose of the lesson; it doesn't stay focused on the skill at hand; it doesn't actively demonstrate how the reading skill is to be applied; it doesn't engage students in the process; and it doesn't close in a way that summarizes their learning. In Teacher B's classroom, on the other hand, each of these instructional elements does take place. These students would most likely be able to say in their own words that they've learned about making predictions and why it is important to a good reader. And if they're able to articulate what they have learned about the skill or strategy, then there's a greater likelihood that they'll take that skill and use it when it counts—in their real reading!

How To Use This Book

Instructional Flexibility

If your school uses a basal reader program for instruction, there are several ways to organize your year using the lessons in this book. You might follow your basal curriculum and consult the table of contents in this book to find a lesson to help you teach the skill/strategy the basal curriculum calls for. Or, you might follow this book, and then use your basal as it meets the text criteria specified for each lesson.

If your school's approach is literature based, you can follow your local curriculum and consult the table of contents in this book to see which lesson correlates with the defined skill/strategy. Or, you can follow this book and use your literature for the context of the lessons, again using the text specifications provided in each lesson to locate appropriate material. You might also choose to use available content texts, including textbooks, so that students will become comfortable with expository text.

No matter how you use this book within your overall reading instruction, it's important to take your local or state curriculum and cross-check it with the table of contents to see if any gaps exist. You'll also be the best person to make the decision about how often a skill or strategy needs to be revisited and reinforced.

Sequencing Your Lessons

For the most part, you can pick and choose lessons randomly throughout the book. We recommend viewing the sections as a menu. You can select lessons appropriately based on your students' needs and on opportunities to integrate lessons with other content being taught.

There are just a few exceptions to this recommendation. First, because Section One deals with basic print and language concepts, its lessons should be included at the beginning of the school year and reinforced until students are comfortable with the basics. Then you'll be ready to branch out far beyond the rudimentary concepts of these lessons.

The other exception is those lessons that are set up purposely in a certain sequence. These are clearly identified as having multiple parts from the start. It's best to look out ahead of time for these lessons so that you won't wind up getting the cart before the horse with activities or with presentation of concepts.

Additional Considerations

There are a few additional key considerations to keep in mind as you approach these lessons and as you consider the best ways you will use them within your overall reading curriculum. Below is a list of some of these considerations:

- What printed text should be used? Many of these lessons suggest specific titles but also provide general guidelines to allow you the freedom to choose what you want to use and to take into consideration the materials that are available in your own teaching situation.

- Is there any vocabulary essential to understanding the printed text you'll be using for a given lesson? You'll want to keep the presentation of vocabulary to a minimum within the context of these mini-lessons, but some words may be critical to preview for students.

- How much support will students need to read the text for a given lesson? Even if a lesson suggests reading the text aloud to your class, you are definitely the best person to decide if a different presentation is called for. Perhaps, for certain lessons and in certain situations, you'll want your students to read chorally with you or with a partner or a small group.

- What will tomorrow's lesson be? You'll base this on the closure from the day's lesson and on feedback from previous lessons. If at the conclusion of a lesson you see that your students "got it" and don't need any clarification, then perhaps you'll choose to focus on another skill or strategy the following day. Or perhaps you'll feel they need a little more—or occasionally a lot more—practice, in which case you'll continue to teach and reteach the current skill or strategy. It's all based on students' needs and the evidence you're able to gather.

- The final point is perhaps the most obvious, but it's too often overlooked in the face of all the other demands confronting teachers, so we feel it's worth underscoring. As you plan each lesson, it's clarifying to ask one simple question of yourself: *What do I need to teach that will help my students become better readers?* A direct answer to that question alone would eliminate many lessons presently taught in our classrooms. Too often we teach lessons that are ends in themselves. The text isn't what it's about at all—it's really about how to read the text. What we need to teach are lessons that become the means to achieve more long-range goals for our students as readers. It is the hope and intent of this book to meet that need.

Constructing Tool Kits

Have you noticed some students in your classroom who can sit quietly, perhaps squirming just a bit, for the full duration of a read-aloud? Surely, you've noticed those others—the ones who tend to be always in motion. They drum their fingers on the desk, chew their pencils, shake their legs, or twist and turn in their seats. These kinesthetic learners actually need to move to learn.

Every classroom includes students at both ends of this spectrum, as well as those in the middle. The lessons in this book promote instruction that taps the different learning styles of all students. You'll find that most lessons offer students the opportunity to be not only mentally engaged in reading but physically/tactilely engaged as well. Something as simple as having students place sticky notes on certain pages or moving a "magic" reading stick across the page can help focus energy and attention. So we've structured these lessons to include a great deal of students' active involvement. Even those students who don't need this extra element to remain engaged in learning can benefit from and enjoy this kind of dynamic interaction with text.

To make these kinds of activities manageable in the classroom, you may want to create simple kits to help maximize the time your students have to devote to their tasks. Your students will love having their very own tool kits, and you'll love seeing how engaged they become as they put the kits to use. To construct the kits, you'll first need a sealable sandwich bag for each student in the classroom. You can easily personalize these bags by printing your students' names on self-adhesive mailing labels and sticking them to the bags. See the example above.

The tools should be introduced gradually so that students are taught the appropriate use of each and so that the tools won't be overwhelming to them in the beginning. Here are some tools that you might choose to include in your students' kits:

- **Sticky Notes** About 12 on a pad per kit will be sufficient for a few lessons.

- **VIP Strips** These are sticky notes that you pre-cut, snipping several times toward the sticky end to form "fingers" that students can tear off as needed to mark text. "VIP" stands for Very Important Points (Hoyt, 1998).

- **Magic Reading Sticks** These are ice-pop sticks or tongue depressors with tips dipped in glue and then in a pretty glitter. Each student needs only one of these for—among many possible uses—tracking print, identifying vocabulary words, and underscoring text clues.

- **Sticky Sticks** These come in packs and look similar to pipe cleaners but have a waxy coating that adheres to book pages. They can cling to a book page and then be stripped away without leaving a residue. They are malleable and also can be cut into smaller strips. They are used to highlight and identify words, phrases, and clues.

- **Pocket Chart Highlighters** These are brightly colored, transparent, flexible plastic strips, approximately 2 inches by 4 inches. They come in packs of about 24 and are useful for highlighting sections of text.

- **Highlighter Pens** These come in a variety of colors and are used to highlight text.

- **Bookmarks** These can be handy as placeholders and can serve double duty to track print or highlight sentences that are discussed. Bookmarks can be purchased, downloaded free from the Internet, or made by students.

- **Response Cards** These are useful in eliciting responses from all students, thereby helping circumvent the frequent classroom phenomenon in which a few students always respond while others remain passive. Each student's tool kit contains one index card with the word *Yes* and another with the word *No*. When you ask a question, all students are to respond with one of the cards.

- **Crayons** A crayon or two can be included for use as highlighters to mark text and for occasional additional uses.

- **Word Frame** For this, you'll use a die-cut template to cut an appealing shape from construction paper. After the figure is cut, snip a small window in the figure. (You might need to fold the figure to make an evenly cut window.) Then, run the figure through your laminator and trim the edges. The result is a fun figure with a window for students to frame words and phrases. See right for one example.

You may think of other items—such as paper clips and index cards to mark pages—to include in the kits as the year progresses. Have fun creating these kits and guiding your students to use them to get more hands-on involved in reading!

Beyond These Lessons

When asked why they're learning to read, many students respond that it's to please the teacher—which in one sense is an admirable answer, but not at all why they need to learn to read! They are also likely to respond that they're learning to read to pass to second grade—again an ambitious goal, but not why we want them to learn to read. We must do two things in addition to teaching the skills and strategies in this book so that students will realize that reading is both a necessary and joyful part of daily life.

First, we must continue to show them the "real-world" purposes served by reading and being literate. That means bringing in real-world reading materials to share and making those available to the students—take-out menus, pet-care booklets, nutrition pamphlets, the school/district newsletter, how-to manuals, dental hygiene and health-care pamphlets, recipe books, newspapers, the school menu, thank-you notes from relatives and friends, postcards we've received, e-mail messages from teachers in other parts of the country, and so many other real-world types of written communication. Students need to see clearly that reading is necessary in our everyday lives.

Second, we need to read aloud to students every single day so that they discover the real joy of reading. You'll help them understand quickly that the squiggly lines on the page do, indeed, have meaning. Read to them often without any lessons connected—just for pure enjoyment. Let them hear the different sounds and patterns of language and the stories and information that will challenge their minds and imaginations.

Good Luck and Enjoy!

Matrix of Standards*

Standards	Lesson Page
Use a variety of strategies to derive meaning from texts	All lessons
Self-monitor comprehension	29, 32, 33, 34, 35, 36, 37, 38, 53, 55, 56, 72, 73, 74, 75, 76, 77
Select books and read independently for extended periods of time to derive pleasure and to gain information	52, 53, 54, 55, 56
Make connections between texts read aloud or independently and prior knowledge, other texts, and the world	31, 43, 49, 52, 82, 83, 84, 85, 86, 87,
Recognize new information as separate from known information in text	31, 32, 34
Establish purposes for reading (to be informed, to follow directions, to be entertained, to use environmental print)	48, 49
Identify the title, author, and illustrator of a text as well as parts of a book (cover, table of contents, title page)	41, 43, 52, 86, 102, 103, 105, 106, 107, 108, 109, 110
Retell stories	36, 53, 61, 68, 69, 73, 90, 91, 92, 94, 95
Recall details in texts read aloud and begin to recall details in texts read independently	36, 50, 53, 62, 63, 65, 77, 90, 91, 92, 94, 95, 96, 97, 98, 99, 111
Use graphic/semantic organizers to organize and categorize information	59, 60, 61, 62, 63, 65, 67, 68, 69, 84, 87
Identify beginning, middle, and end of a story	91, 92, 94
Identify text that uses sequence or other logical order	68, 69, 92, 94, 111
Ask and answer questions about texts read aloud	41, 43, 44, 45, 46, 48, 49, 50, 51, 52, 53, 54, 55, 56
Use pictures and words to make predictions about stories read aloud or independently	41, 43, 46, 48, 49, 50, 51, 52, 54, 83, 84, 85, 86, 87
Create mental images when reading and compose visual images from what is read	72, 73, 74, 75, 76, 77, 78, 79, 92
Use content (specialized) vocabulary	73, 96, 107, 108, 109
Confirm predictions (by identifying key words/signpost words)	41, 46, 83, 84, 85, 86, 87, 96, 109
Draw conclusions and make inferences	54, 58, 99
Categorize and classify words and ideas	46, 60, 61, 62, 63, 65, 67, 68, 69, 95, 96, 105, 106, 107, 108, 109, 110, 111, 113, 114
Begin to summarize main ideas in texts read aloud or independently	58, 73, 92, 94, 95, 96, 97, 98, 99
Respond to questions of *who, what, why, when, where,* and *how*	23, 44, 51

Standards	Lesson Page
Begin to distinguish between fact and fantasy in texts read aloud or independently	35
Begin to use graphic representations such as charts, graphs, pictures, and graphic organizers as information sources and as a means of organizing information and events logically; use them to perform a task	35, 59, 60, 61, 62, 63, 65, 67, 68, 69, 73, 76, 84, 87, 96, 111
Respond to texts through a variety of methods, such as creative dramatics, writing, and graphic art	45, 73, 75, 78, 90, 91, 92, 94, 98, 102, 103, 105, 106
Begin to compare and contrast information, ideas, and elements within a single text	65
Compare and contrast similarities and differences between two texts	65
Identify basic story elements—characters, setting, and simple plot—in a literary work	37, 59, 60, 61, 62, 63, 65
Analyze characters (traits, feelings, relationships, changes)	37, 99
Begin to identify problem and solution in a work of fiction or drama	62, 63
Begin to identify devices of figurative language, such as similes and metaphors	79
Identify the characteristics of genres such as fiction, poetry, drama, and informational texts, as well as the characteristics of newsletters, lists, and signs; tell the difference between fiction and nonfiction	35, 65, 102, 103, 105, 106, 107, 108, 110, 111, 113, 114
Read widely from different genres	All lessons
Respond to text in writing and through acting	91, 92, 98, 102
Develop vocabulary through meaningful/concrete experiences	48, 67, 74, 75, 76, 77, 90, 107, 108, 109
Use basic elements of phonetic analysis (hear, segment, substitute, blend sounds, recognize and make use of visual cues, onset, and patterns)	20, 21, 22, 23, 24, 26
Recognize conventions used in printed sentences and for comprehension	22, 23, 26, 44, 51, 114
Use structural clues and common spelling patterns to decode and understand text	24, 25, 38, 107
Use context clues to construct meaning	38
Read aloud smoothly, easily, and expressively in familiar text (employing proper pacing, phrasing, intonation, and rhythm)	18, 24, 26, 55, 114
Use resources and references to build upon word meanings	107, 108, 109
Use simple reference materials to obtain information (books, dictionaries, software, and parts of those books—tables of contents, chapter titles, guide words, indices)	41, 43, 52, 86, 102, 103, 105, 106, 107, 108, 109, 110
Use alphabetical order to locate information	96, 97, 107, 108
Recognize rhyme, rhythm, and patterned structures in children's text	113
Apply concepts of print when reading • Read top to bottom, left to right • Know common sight words, including compound words and contractions • Match oral words to printed words • Identify that meaningful text is made up of sentences, words, and letters	18, 24, 19, 20 21, 22, 23

*Along with the National Standards, the standards of the following eleven states were gathered to create the curriculum for this book: California, Colorado, Florida, Indiana, Missouri, New York, Pennsylvania, South Carolina, Texas, Virginia, and Washington.

Section One

Applying Basic Print Concepts

We can't take for granted that first graders come to us with the necessary foundation that will make them successful in their early attempts at reading. Although all students have had exposure to spoken language, many students entering first grade lack a basic knowledge of print concepts—concepts unique to written language and dramatically different in structure from oral language. The lessons in this section are intended to familiarize your students with these concepts during the early part of the year.

Imagine how it feels to be confronted with page after page of what appear to be lots of squiggly, meaningless lines! This is the experience of many beginning first graders. So, in the classroom we start with the most basic components of text: we explain how to hold a book, how to identify the top of the page and the bottom, and why readers must move their eyes from left to right as they decode print. Once that foundation has been laid, we advance to distinguishing among letters, words, and sentences, and we demonstrate how these elements come together to create whole text. (Note: Although outside the purview of this book, some form of phonics instruction should occur in concert with these early print concept lessons.)

Reading is really all about thinking, and that's why, from Section Two lessons through the end of this book, our focus is on understanding and comprehension. Our very first job, however, is to enable our youngest students to grasp the fundamentals of print and language, to provide them with the joy of being read aloud to, and to help them understand that reading is purposeful to their lives. These are the basics we address here in Section One. While not an end unto themselves, they are the critical tools that will allow us to achieve our ultimate goal—having students independently gain meaning from text.

What a joyous occasion we celebrate, when a student first makes sense of those squiggly marks on the page! We can see ahead a lifetime of wonderful literacy experiences.

This teacher is helping her students to sort through the dialogue in a book by using differently colored tape to indicate the words spoken by different characters.

A first-grade teacher has used students' names on a Word Wall to help her class explore letters, sounds, and words in the beginning of the year.

READING TOP TO BOTTOM AND LEFT TO RIGHT

Explanation

At the beginning of the school year, we can't take anything for granted about how rich students' literacy experiences have been. This lesson is truly for beginners. Once you have introduced these activities to your class, you can use them daily to start your reading and to help students track print during whole-class read-alouds.

Skill Focus

Applying basic concepts of print when reading: reading top to bottom and left to right

Materials & Resources

Text

- Any simple Big Book appropriate for emergent readers

Other

- A pointer

Bonus Ideas

- If your class is ready, you might put both sets of movements (top, bottom; left, right) together in one song. You might even repeat the song several times—speeding up each time until it's impossible to keep the pace!
- For a brief activity to help ease a transition during the school day, try a simple game of Simon Says. Use the directions *top, bottom, left, and right* to help students become even more familiar with the words. Remind students again that these are directions their eyes will need to help them become good readers.

STEPS

1. Tell students that today the class will do some "reading exercises" together. Have them stand in the meeting area you use for class read-alouds. Ask them to put their hands above their heads and reach for the sky on their tiptoes. Say, "We're reaching to the top, boys and girls." Then have students drop their hands, bend, and touch the floor. Tell them, "We're dropping to the bottom, boys and girls."

2. Repeat both actions several times while students say *top* and *bottom* as they reach up and down.

3. Now put this exercise to music—to the familiar tune of "This is the way we...." Sing and do the following motions several times:

   (Hands on hips)
   This is the way we
   read our books
   Read our books, read our books

   This is the way we
   read our books
   (Reach high and then low)
   From the top to the bottom.

4. Tell students you've got something to add to the song. It's another important message they need to learn about how to read. To avoid confusion about left and right orientation, turn so that students are behind you. With hands on your hips, lean far to the left and say, "This is the left." Next lean far to the right and say, "Now I'm leaning far to the right." Do this a few times as you repeat the words *left* and *right*.

5. Repeat both actions several times while students say *left* and *right* as they lean left and right.

6. Repeat the activity described in Step 3 but substitute the following line at the end of the verse:

   (Sway to the left and then the right) From the left to the right.

7. Gather students near you and display the Big Book. Tell them that even though their bodies are tired from the exercise, their eyes might still be able to do the same exercise. Explain that readers' eyes always start at the top of a page and read to the bottom as you sweep your pointer from the top to the bottom of the page. Next, explain that readers read each line from left to right. Take your pointer and sweep left to right on each line of text on one page.

8. Tell students you're going to read to them as you move the pointer from top to bottom and left to right. You want them to give their eyes some exercise: their job is to follow the pointer. Read the book aloud, moving the pointer as you go. Ask occasionally, "Will our eyes start at the top or the bottom of the page?" and "Will our eyes start on the left or the right on this line?"

MATCHING ORAL WORDS TO PRINTED WORDS

Explanation

As emerging readers begin to match oral words to printed words, they are taking a big step toward reading. In this lesson, we'll call attention to the fact that written language–just like spoken language–is composed of individual units called words. And at some point in this lesson, it's also valuable to remind students that all the little words they're pointing to will tell them some wonderful stories this year!

Skill Focus

Applying basic concepts of print when reading: matching oral words to printed words

Materials & Resources

Text

- Any simple Big Book appropriate for emergent readers; multiple copies of the same Big Book in small-book format (optional)

Other

- A pointer

Bonus Ideas

Here are three ideas for pointers:

- A colorful gardening glove stuffed with polyfiber (hot-glue the thumb and three fingers to the palm, leaving the pointer finger extended; use yarn to attach to a dowel at the wrist)
- A dowel rod with the tip dipped in glue and in glitter and/or attached to a bauble
- A flyswatter with a portion of the flap cut out to form a frame for words

Note: *This lesson offers an ideal time to present each student with a magic reading stick—a personal pointer that they can use all year. (See page 12.)*

STEPS

1. Explain to students that individual words make up what we say and what we read. Readers can easily recognize words on a book page because the words have spaces around them.
2. Read the Big Book through once, using your pointer to track the print as you read aloud. Instead of sweeping the pointer underneath the words, pick up the pointer and place it on each word individually as you read. (See Bonus Ideas for pointer tips.)
3. Read the book through a second time, now inviting any students who feel comfortable doing so to read along with you. Again guide the reading with your pointer—picking it up and placing it on each word.
4. Reread a particularly interesting page. Ask students to count the words on this page with you as you indicate each one.
5. Now ask students to count the spaces between words with you as you point to those.
6. Pass the pointer to a student and ask that student to point to each word on that same page as the class counts the words.
7. You might conclude the lesson by distributing multiple copies of the Big Book in small-book format. Engage the class in a choral reading of the text to allow them the opportunity to use their magic reading sticks (see Note above). Have them "touch" the words during the choral reading. Stop the reading occasionally to make sure that everyone is pointing to the correct word.

MATCHING ORAL WORDS TO PRINTED WORDS (KINESTHETICALLY)

Explanation

In this lesson, we'll continue to reinforce the basic concept of matching oral words to printed words. This time, however, we'll encourage students to engage kinesthetically with the words. Actually holding an individual word in their hands will help many students grasp the concept that words are separate entities that come together to form sentences.

Skill Focus

Applying basic concepts of print when reading: matching oral words to printed words

Materials & Resources

Text

- Big Book used in previous lesson

Other

- Several sentence strips
- Scissors
- Pocket chart

Bonus Ideas

Once students are familiar with this activity, repeat it with a different sentence. This time, however, invite different volunteers to play the role of teacher–to use the pointer, to distribute word cards, to tap students, and so on.

STEPS

1. Reread the book used in the previous lesson, using your pointer to track the print. Pick up the pointer and lightly place it on each of the words as you read them.
2. Read the book through a second time, now inviting any students who feel comfortable doing so to read along with you. Again guide the reading with your pointer—picking it up and placing it on each word.
3. Choose a sentence from the book, write it on a sentence strip, and place the sentence strip in the pocket chart. Read the sentence aloud as you tap each word with your pointer.
4. Now have volunteers come forward and take turns "tapping" the words as you all read the sentence together.
5. Next rewrite the same sentence on another sentence strip and cut apart the individual words. In the correct sentence order, place each word in the pocket chart underneath the intact sentence strip. Reread the sentence with students.
6. Hand each separate word to a different student. Point, in order, to the words in the sentence that remains in the pocket chart. Ask the student with the indicated word to come forward and display the word for the class. Continue until the whole sentence is represented. Be sure that the students are arranged in the correct order so that the seated students will be able to read from left to right.
7. Stand behind students who are holding the words and tap each lightly on the shoulder. Have students who are seated read the word displayed by each tapped student until the entire sentence has been read aloud.
8. Tell each student holding a word to give that word to a seated classmate. Call the new group of students forward and repeat the activity. Continue until all students have had an opportunity to hold a word.

IDENTIFYING THAT WORDS ARE MADE UP OF LETTERS

Explanation

Students need to understand that the smallest unit of print is a letter. As part of their phonics work, students will eventually learn the sound relationships that correspond with these units. In the English language, that's where things get a bit complicated! But in this lesson we are primarily concerned with reinforcing the basic concept that words are composed of letters.

Skill Focus

Applying basic concepts of print when reading: identifying that words are made of letters

Materials & Resources

Text

- Any simple Big Book appropriate for emergent readers

Other

- Several sentence strips
- Scissors
- Pocket chart (you might use the same sentence strips and pocket charts from the two previous lessons)

Bonus Ideas

To reinforce the concept of this lesson, use this literacy center idea. Type your students' first names. Use a large font that students can read easily. Print two copies of all the names and cut them apart into strips. For each name, leave one strip intact and cut the other into its individual letters. Package each pair of names in a sandwich bag. Students will enjoy recreating their name and their friends' names!

STEPS

1. If you're starting with a new Big Book (rather than continuing with the Big Book used in the previous two lessons), introduce the book's subject and do a shared reading of the text using your pointer to guide the print. Read the book to students once, and then invite them to join you in a second reading.

2. Write a particularly interesting sentence on a sentence strip, explicitly stretching out the sounds as you write the words. Place the sentence strip in the pocket chart.

3. Using your pointer, read the sentence aloud. Lift the pointer each time you read a new word.

4. Pass the pointer to different students and invite them to guide the class in rereading the sentence.

5. Now cut the sentence into its individual words and hand the words to different children.

6. As you read the sentence from the text (or say it from memory), have students come forward to place their word in the correct sequence in the chart. This will help students remember that the sentence is made up of words.

7. With all the words in place in the chart, select one—preferably a high-frequency word that is phonetically proper—and remove it. Explain that all words are made of individual letters and that you will prove this. Cut the word into its letters. Hand each individual letter to a student.

8. Invite these students to help you put the word back together. Have students come forward with appropriate letters, placing them back in the correct order to re-form the word within the sentence in the pocket chart.

9. Follow these same steps for several of the words, rereading the sentence each time the word is properly re-formed on the chart.

Identifying That Text Is Made Up of Sentences

Explanation

This lesson begins instruction about the concept that text is composed of sentences. Most first graders require a good deal of exposure to models (both in their own reading and in what is read to them) before they acquire a true sense of what makes up a sentence. But it will and does happen—be patient and keep modeling!

Skill Focus

Applying basic concepts of print when reading: identifying that text is made of sentences

Materials & Resources

Text

- A typical Morning Message

Other

- Chart or board on which Morning Message is written
- 3 different colored markers

Bonus Ideas

As an auxiliary to this lesson, have students count the number of lines of text that they see. Point out that end marks don't necessarily occur at the end of a line but rather at the end of a thought. Carefully distinguish between a line and a complete sentence so that students learn the difference.

Steps

1. On the chalkboard or poster paper, write your regular Morning Message for students. Plan your message to include all three types of end punctuation marks. Here is a sample:

   Dear Class,
   Today we will learn many new things! We will read a good story about spiders. We will go to PE with Mrs. Jumper. We will use finger paints, too. I like to paint. Do you? I know we will all have fun!
   Love,
   Mrs. Lovett

2. Use your pointer as you read the message aloud to students. Reread the message, this time inviting students to read along with you.

3. Tell students you want them to hunt for marks that are different from words. These marks show that the writer has said a complete thought that makes sense. Demonstrate the three marks that end a sentence by writing them on the board or chart: **. ! ?** As you write each, identify it by its correct name: "a period," "an exclamation mark," "a question mark." Tell students that these marks give us important information about a sentence; they'll learn more about that information shortly. But for now their job is simply to locate the marks.

4. Using one colored marker (for example, red), invite students to hunt for periods with you. As the class identifies a period, draw a large circle around it with the marker.

5. Using a different colored marker (for example, green), have students hunt for exclamation marks. Again, circle each. Follow the same procedure, using a third color, for question marks.

6. On the board, create a simple chart. A sample is at right:

End Marks We Found	Number
Periods	4
Exclamation Marks	2
Question Marks	1
Total	7

7. Using your pointer, return to the Morning Message and count the end punctuation marks. Write the total number at the end of your message. Point out that this number is the same as the total number on the chart. Explain that what you have just identified is the total number of complete sentences in your Morning Message.

IDENTIFYING THAT TEXT IS MADE UP OF LETTERS, WORDS, AND SENTENCES

Explanation

Until students have a firm grasp of the basics, you'll need to repeat lessons similar to this one to reinforce the concept that meaningful text is composed of letters, words, and sentences. This lesson also gives students some practice in counting.

Skill Focus

Applying basic concepts of print when reading: identifying that meaningful text is made of sentences, words, and letters

Materials & Resources

Text

- A typical Morning Message

Other

- Chart or board on which Morning Message is written
- 3 different colored markers

Bonus Ideas

You can create a quick and easy center activity based on this lesson. After writing your daily Morning Message, provide a chart, pointer, and pencil for students. Invite them to record the number of letters, lines, words, different end punctuation marks, and sentences in the Message. At a later point students can compute the results.

STEPS

1. On the chalkboard or poster paper, write your regular Morning Message for students. A sample follows:
   Dear Class,
   We will be busy learning today. We will read about seasons. We will practice counting by 5's. Also, we will go to the library today. I'm glad that you are here!
   Love,
   Mrs. Lovett

2. Use your pointer as you read the message aloud to students. Reread the message, this time inviting students to read along with you.

3. Ask students to count the number of sentences with you (five in the sample above, not including greeting and sign-off). Use a colored marker to write that number at the end of the piece. Circle the number.

4. Next, count the number of words in each sentence. Use a different colored marker to write the appropriate number directly following each sentence. Circle the numbers.

5. Next, count the number of letters in each word in at least one sentence. Use a third colored marker to write the number of letters above each word. Circle the numbers.

6. Write these words on the board:
   letters words lines sentences

   Now ask several questions aloud. (Select from the list below.) Invite students to think and talk about the answers as you pose them. You might allow students to turn and talk to a buddy before responding. You might also ask a volunteer to come and point to the correct answer once it's established. These questions will be thought-provoking for emergent readers. Give them time to think!
   - Which of these do we have the most of in our Morning Message?
   - Which of these do we have the fewest of in our Morning Message?
   - Do we have more lines or more sentences?
   - Do we have more letters or more words?
   - Can we have words without letters?
   - Can we have letters without words?
   - Can we have sentences without letters?
   - Can we have sentences without words?
   - In everything that we read, what do you think we'll have the most of? Why?

USING COMMON SIGHT WORDS TO DEVELOP FLUENCY

Explanation

Once students read and write basic high-frequency words automatically, reading and writing are easier for them and they accomplish both with greater fluidity. The other benefit is that their brains are then free to attend to the more difficult aspects of reading and writing—comprehension and craft. Many teachers create Word Walls to help students build sight vocabulary. This lesson suggests an alternate idea.

Skill Focus

Knowing common sight words; reading aloud smoothly, easily, and expressively in familiar text

Materials & Resources

Text

- Transparency of a few pages of simple text that includes many high-frequency words

Other

- Markers; paste; scissors; hole puncher
- For each student: 1 file folder, 1 sheet protector; 1 sheet unlined paper; 2 pipe cleaners, 1 keyboard print from Appendix, page 116 (Note: It's best to laminate the laptops)

Bonus Ideas

At different points, tell the class which words to write and have them practice typing the words together, just as in today's lesson. Other times give them individual words that they need to specifically learn or practice. In any case, they should always have their laptops available!

STEPS

1. Using the transparency, read aloud the sample text you've prepared. Invite students to read it aloud with you a second time.

2. Using your transparency pen, underline or highlight all the words that you consider to be high-frequency words. These words should make up the majority of the text. You might say, "These are the words that you'll see most often in your reading and that you'll need to use (not just want to use!) in your writing. Teachers call these words 'high-frequency words.' It's important for you to learn to read and write these words correctly."

3. Stress to students that accuracy with *all* words certainly isn't expected at this point. High-frequency words aid fluency so greatly, however, that using them correctly is a real goal. Tell students that you have a surprise for each of them. It will help them to learn these special words that are so important in their growth as readers.

4. Give each student a file folder into which you've punched four holes for the "handles" of the "laptop," along with two pipe cleaners and the keyboard. (Refer to the diagram below.) Provide these directions:
   - Attach the pipe cleaners with a twist after threading through the holes.
   - Attach the sheet protector as the laptop "screen."
   - Cut out the keyboard carefully and paste it on the inside bottom panel in the position that a laptop keyboard would be placed.

5. Select three or four high-frequency words you've read in the sample text. Guide students to write these carefully on the unlined paper and then insert in the "monitor."

6. Model for students how to open their laptops, position their hands, and then pretend to type out a word (the hunt-and-peck method is fine!). Select one high-frequency word from the sample text and have students "type" it three times, spelling it aloud as they type. Continue until the class has typed all key words in the sample.

7. Use this procedure often (in different subject lessons, as well as reading lessons) for high-frequency words that students don't read or write automatically. The practice and repetition will help!

USING STRUCTURAL CLUES TO DECODE AND UNDERSTAND

Explanation

First-grade students need to be aware of word features that provide clues about meaning. This awareness will help them in their development of text comprehension, the underlying goal of all reading. Capitalizing on visuals, this lesson provides a fun way to explore compound words, contractions, and words with common prefixes or suffixes.

Skill Focus

Using structural cues to decode and understand text

Materials & Resources

Text

- Sample text that includes numerous compound words, contractions, or common prefixes/suffixes (Suggested for this lesson: *The Quicksand Book* by Tomie dePaola, which provides examples of all three categories)

Other

- Marker
- 2 sheets of unlined paper cut into quarters (widthwise and lengthwise)
- For each student: 1 sheet of unlined paper cut in half widthwise and lengthwise

Bonus Ideas

Use this same activity to explore other word parts such as prefixes and contractions.

STEPS

1. Read the selected text aloud to students or with students.
2. Read the text again, this time calling attention to the category of words you'll emphasize for this lesson. (We recommend choosing just one category per lesson so as not to confuse first graders.) For example, if you are using the suggested book, you might choose the word *quicksand* from its title. Write the word on the board or on a transparency. Ask students if they notice little words within this big word. Guide them to the two words—*quick* and *sand*, which students will likely recognize and understand separately. Discuss students' understandings of these individual words.
3. Explain that this big word made of two separate words is called a *compound word*. Write the word *compound* and tell students that it means something that has been 'mixed together.' Ask them what two things chocolate milk is made of. When they likely respond, "Chocolate syrup and milk," tell them that's the same way that compound words are made—by mixing two words together to make a new word.
4. Now write on the board or a transparency all the compound words you find on several pages of the selected text—for example, *underground*, *riverbed*, and *watertight*.
5. Fold in half lengthwise one of the cut sections of paper (see Materials & Resources: each cut section should be one-quarter of a sheet of standard paper). Lift the top flap and write one of the compound words in big letters. At the point where the two words come together, snip the top flap to the crease as shown in the diagram in Step 6.
6. Take turns opening each flap and asking students to identify the first and last words separately. Then open the entire flap and have students read the compound word. See diagram:

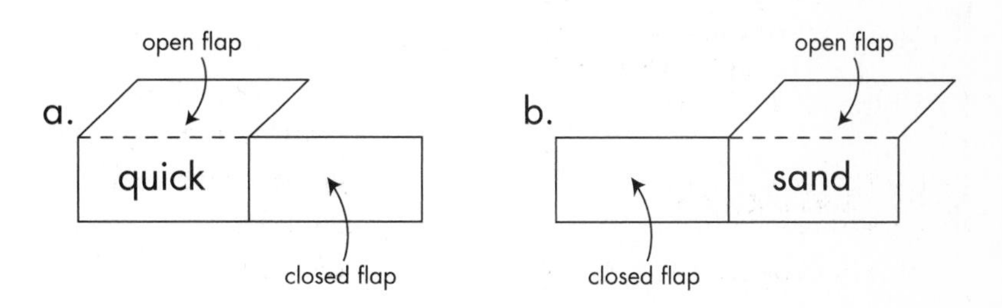

7. Have students write the remaining words on their own papers in this same manner. Then group students into pairs and have partners quiz each other about the separate word parts and the whole compound word (following your model).

READING ALOUD A "FIST-FULL" FLUENTLY

Explanation

At first with your guidance and then on their own, students practice reading with expression and accuracy. This lesson provides a format that you'll want to use often in your reading instruction. It offers a gradual release of responsibility from teacher to student as it fosters development of good reading habits.

Skill Focus

Reading aloud smoothly, easily, and expressively in familiar text

Materials & Resources

Text

- Simple fiction or nonfiction text in multiple copies or Big Book format (Suggested for this lesson: *Kitten's First Full Moon* by Kevin Henkes)

Bonus Ideas

Use the "fist-full" technique as a meaningful filler activity for students who have finished their work early. Allow them to "perform" their excerpt at an appropriate free moment.

STEPS

1. Discuss with students that being a good reader means reading accurately and with expression. When good readers read, they sound almost like they're just having a conversation. To accomplish this, readers have to practice a great deal. They have to read a lot and hear others read. Assure students that they'll all have a chance to practice their reading in this lesson.

2. Ask students to listen carefully to you as you read the selection for the first time. (Be sure to practice ahead what you're going to read so that you provide an excellent fluency model.) Pay close attention to punctuation marks, pauses, and any significant words that should cause you to change the inflection in your voice. In *Kitten's First Full Moon*, you might want to exaggerate some of the verbs related to the kitten to emphasize its actions—*pulled*, *wiggled*, *sprang*, and *tumbled*.

3. Ask students to evaluate your reading. If you made any errors, be frank in admitting them and offer your own analysis of why those errors may have occurred.

4. Now have students read along with you for a second and, perhaps, a third reading. Stop periodically to discuss how a good reader would approach fluency on a particular page.

5. When you feel students have practiced sufficiently with your guidance, invite each student to find a "fist-full" of text (or a "pinch" if the type size of the text you're using is small) to practice reading. Direct them to ball up a fist and place it on the printed page, practicing all the lines within that span (or within the span of their fingers pinched together if type is small). Give them time to read over their selected text several times. Have them practice until they have achieved complete fluency. Circulate around the room to monitor and support students who need additional help.

6. Invite students to "perform" for the class the text they've practiced. If necessary, continue this lesson for another day until everyone has had a chance to read to the class. Take every opportunity to praise students' efforts as they build confidence in this activity, which will represent for many a memorable early "real reading" experience.

Section Two

Monitoring Comprehension

Too often students pick up a book and engage in what seems like reading. However, what is actually happening is that they are "calling" words. They may be calling words with accuracy and clarity and they may do so from the start to the finish of a whole book, but if they are not understanding what the words mean, they are not really reading. Genuine reading is a complex process that involves a multitude of cognitive activities. Put most succinctly, reading is thinking.

In *I Read It, but I Don't Get It!*, Cris Tovani (2000) calls attention to the fact that we have two voices that work in tandem during reading—one voice saying the words and one responding to the words. Readers have to activate both voices in order to be successfully, genuinely reading. Some students don't do this automatically. They need direct instruction to become aware of the intricacies of reading.

The lessons in this section teach first graders to be metacognitive, or self-aware, in their reading. The research of Harris and Hodges (1995) defines this as "knowing when what one is reading makes sense by monitoring and controlling one's own comprehension" (p. 39). In fact, one of our paramount goals for young readers is helping them to become aware of their own thinking during reading.

These lessons will help students become keenly aware that as they read they will have a great variety of experiences. Sometimes they will encounter things they already know but often they will discover new knowledge. This knowledge may fit nicely with what they already know, but sometimes it will surprise them and/or even puzzle them. These activities are all central to reading. Students need to be equipped to realize that if none of this is happening at a given point or during a given piece of text, they may have stopped thinking. They need to be able to recognize that this is a problem and they need to have ready strategies to resolve the situation. Then, and only then, will they be in control of their ability to navigate text successfully.

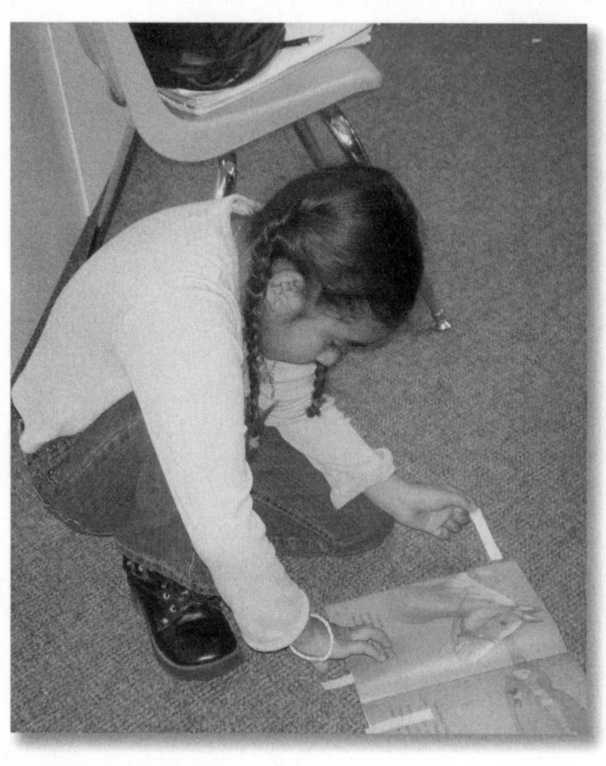

This girl is using sticky notes to mark new knowledge in the text she's reading.

These five magic reading sticks have been decorated with glitter at the tips to make reading even more fun for first graders!

TURNING THE READING SWITCH ON

Explanation

Many beginning readers have not learned the true purpose of reading—that the reader must go beyond merely decoding words to make sense of the text. This lesson introduces that concept in a unique way!

Skill Focus

Using a variety of strategies to derive meaning from texts; self-monitoring comprehension

Materials & Resources

Text

- Any grade-appropriate narrative or informational text of about five to six sentences (Sample used in this lesson is adapted from *A Look at Spiders* by J. Halpern)

Other

- Chalkboard or overhead transparency

STEPS

1. Announce that you're going to draw something and you hope students will be able to guess what it is. (Let's hope for a good artistic day!) Slowly sketch a silhouette of a person's head. Tell students to raise their hands when they think they can identify the picture.

2. Once students have identified correctly what you've drawn, ask them if they can guess what you're putting inside the head. Give them this clue: It is something we all have. Within the silhouette, draw the outline of a brain. (See example in Step 3.)

3. When students have guessed correctly, tell them that we all have a switch in our brains that we have to learn to turn on when we read. Explain that good readers know about this important switch. Draw a switch and label it with "on" and "off." See example below:

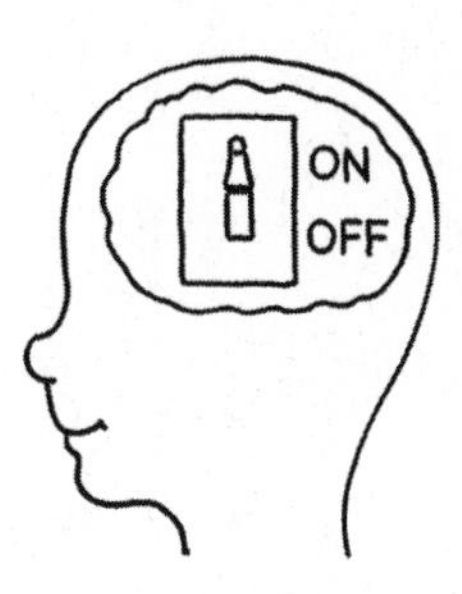

4. Tell students that you want them to pay special attention as you read a passage twice. Their job is to notice the difference between a reader who has the switch "on" and one who has the switch "off." First, you'll read the passage without turning the switch on. Using the sample in the first column in the chart on page 30, or any comparable text, read the words without any think-aloud comments. At the end of your reading, make an observation like that at the end of the middle column.

5. Now tell students you're going to click the "on" switch. This time you'll interact with the text and share with the class what you're thinking. Read the same text again, adding comments like those in the third column.

6. Have students discuss the differences in the two readings. Challenge them to phrase in their own words the benefits of reading the way you did the second time. Invite students to use the "on" switch in their brains today while they read. After they finish reading (either an assigned text or an independent choice), have students share some of what they thought about while reading. Ask them to describe what it felt like to deliberately turn that switch on!

Mini-Lesson

Sample Text to Read Aloud	Directions and Suggested Conversation for First Reading (without switch "on")	Directions and Suggested Conversation for Second Reading (with switch "on")
Spiders have a very interesting way of eating. What they eat may surprise you! (1) They chew their food and turn it into a liquid. (2) Then they drink the food just like a milkshake! (3) Some spiders will eat other spiders. (4) Most eat small insects like moths and crickets. In all, they eat about 2,000 insects a year! (5) Big tarantulas can even eat small animals! (6)	[Slowly and without much inflection read the words. Don't speak until after you've finished reading the entire passage.] After reading, make a comment like this: "This passage was pretty interesting, but I wasn't really thinking about it while I was reading so all I know is it had something to do with spiders eating."	[Read aloud with a thoughtful tone. Insert think-aloud commentary during your reading at the points indicated by numbers in parentheses. Stop when you reach the numbers and make comments like those that follow.] (1) "I know some things about spiders, but I've never thought about how they eat." (2) "I didn't know they turned food into a liquid. That's pretty interesting!" (3) "I know what that's like because I've had a milkshake before. I guess spiders suck up the liquid and maybe it's thick—kind of like a milkshake." (4) "That's pretty gross that spiders will eat each other. I don't think many animals or insects do that." (5) "Wow! 2,000 is a lot!" (6) "I know that tarantulas are huge, hairy spiders. I saw one at the zoo once." End with, "My reading switch was definitely on while I read about spiders. I was thinking the whole time!"

RECOGNIZING SOMETHING I ALREADY KNOW

Explanation

Just about every time we read, we encounter things that are familiar to us. In fact, building on our prior knowledge and incorporating new information into that knowledge is the heart of reading comprehension. In this lesson, students will learn to recognize the familiar in what they read.

Skill Focus

Making connections between texts and prior knowledge

Materials & Resources

Text

- Any grade-appropriate informational short text (Used in this lesson: text adapted from www.enchantedlearning.com)

Other

- 1 VIP strip (see page 12)
- Scissors
- For each student: 1 sticky note

STEPS

1. Tell students that in all informational texts that we read we find many things we already know. We also discover much new information. As they read, good readers are always thinking about putting together what they already know with the new information that they're just learning. Explain that in today's lesson students will get a chance to see how this process works.

2. Model for students how you acknowledge what you already know in text that you read. With your VIP strips in one hand, begin to read a section of text. Whenever you encounter something you already knew before reading this particular text, place a "finger" of the sticky note on that part of the text and model your thought process as you do so. Below is a short text excerpt, accompanied by a teacher's think-aloud. The parenthetical numbers in the text are included to indicate where the teacher stops, thinks aloud, and places a sticky finger. Conclude by saying something like, "There's a lot of new information in this piece, but I can see, too, how many things that I already knew!"

3. Have students cut their sticky notes into fingers, following your model. Then tell them to use their VIP strips during independent or assigned text reading. Just as you did in the modeling, they are to place their sticky fingers at spots where they can say to themselves, "Oh, that's something I already knew before reading this!" At the end of the lesson, call on several students to share something they've marked with a sticky finger.

Sample Text to Read Aloud	Teacher's Think-Aloud at Marked Places in Text
Giant pandas are called bears, but they are quite different from regular bears. For one thing, they have a very special look. They are white with patches of black around their eyes, ears, shoulders, chest, legs, and feet. (1) They don't roar like regular bears. Instead, they are mostly silent but can make several different calls. Pandas don't hibernate or sleep all winter like regular bears. (2) That's because they have food available all year. (3) Also, unlike regular bears, pandas can't walk on their hind legs. They walk on all four legs.	(1) "I already knew what pandas look like. I've seen them in pictures, and I've seen them at the zoo before." (2) "I've read before that pandas don't hibernate, so I knew this interesting fact." (3) "I remember reading somewhere else that pandas eat bamboo, and it grows all year so they always have food."

RECOGNIZING SOMETHING NEW

Explanation

As we examined in the previous lesson, reading comprehension blends the known with the new. If conceptualized as a formula, reading comprehension would look like this: old knowledge + new knowledge = comprehension. We've already explored the prior knowledge students bring to their reading; here we teach them to focus on new knowledge. Since one of the primary purposes for reading is to gain knowledge, this is an important exercise for young readers.

Skill Focus

Recognizing and gaining new knowledge from text

Materials & Resources

Text

- Any grade-appropriate informational short text (Recommended: the text you used in the previous lesson)

Other

- 2 VIP strips made from sticky notes in two different colors
- For each student: 1 sticky note

Bonus Ideas

Occasionally give students an index card prior to reading. Have them write *old* on one side and *new* on the other. Instruct them to jot down something old and something new that they discover during their reading.

STEPS

1. Remind students that in the previous lesson they focused on what they already knew in an informational text selection. Today they will focus on the other side of knowledge: new information. Start by reading the selection and flagging the things that you already know with the "fingers" of your sticky note. (Note that if you are using the same text employed in the previous lesson, it's still valuable to reread and re-mark the same spots. This will provide reinforcement for students.) Once you've used all your strips or you've finished the text, proclaim, "Wow! Look at all of the things I already knew in this text! I think that'll make it easier for me to understand."

2. Now read back through the same paragraph and model the process of discovering new information. Have available VIP strips in different colors from those used in Step 1. Whenever you encounter something you did not already know, place a "finger" of the sticky note on that part of the text and model your thought process as you do so. Below is a short text excerpt, accompanied by a teacher's think-aloud. The parenthetical numbers in the text are included to indicate where the teacher stops, thinks aloud, and places a sticky finger.

Sample Text to Read Aloud	Teacher's Think-Aloud at Marked Places in Text
Giant pandas are called bears, but they are quite different from regular bears. For one thing, they have a very special look. They are white with patches of black around their eyes, ears, shoulders, chest, legs, and feet. They don't roar like regular bears. (1) Instead, they are mostly silent but can make several different calls. Pandas don't hibernate or sleep all winter like regular bears. That's because they have food available all year. Also, unlike regular bears, pandas can't walk on their hind legs. They walk on all four legs. (2)	(1) "I've never even thought about the sound that pandas make. I guess I thought they roared like regular bears." (2) "Here's something else I'm learning by reading this. I've seen lots of pictures and movies where bears stood on their hind legs, but pandas can't do that. That makes them different."

3. Conclude by saying something like, "Well, I've found several things I already knew but also several new things from reading this. I like learning new things!"

4. Display the marked text for the class. Point out the mixture of known and new information identified in the text. Sum up by saying, "Boys and girls, this is how we make sense of what we read. We blend together information that we already know with new information. That's what reading is all about!"

5. Have students cut their sticky notes into fingers, following your model. Then tell them to use their VIP strips during independent or assigned text reading. Just as you did in the modeling, they are to place their sticky fingers at spots where they discover something they did not know before. At the end of the lesson, call on several students to share something they've marked with a sticky finger.

Making a WOW! Discovery

Explanation

As we read, our brains sort through and file information in different ways. Some new information in text is easy to retain while some is not. Like other experiences in life, information that surprises or impresses us in a particular way—that "wows" us—tends to be easier to remember. This lesson introduces students to this concept and gives them a way to recognize these "wow" discoveries.

Skill Focus

Retaining new information from reading

Materials & Resources

Text

- Any grade-appropriate informational text that includes interesting details or facts

Other

- For each student: 1 sheet of unlined paper

Steps

1. Describe for students several experiences in your own life that caused you to stop and exclaim, "Wow!", "Neat!", or "Cool!" Maybe you saw a shooting star as you were driving at night. Perhaps you observed a gorgeous sunset or spotted a sand dollar as you walked on the beach. Ask students if they, too, can remember a time they experienced a "wow" moment and invite a few students to share these moments.

2. Tell students that we also have "wow" moments in our reading. It can happen in fiction as well as when we read nonfiction or informational text. A "wow" reading moment occurs when we encounter something new that takes us by surprise. A character might do something we didn't predict would happen. Or we might read a neat fact that amazes us. Explain that this lesson will help students identify things that surprise or wow them during reading.

3. Write the letters *W-O-W* on the board or on a transparency, making the O large enough to write inside. (See diagram of a reduced version in Step 4.)

4. Read aloud a piece of text, modeling your thinking as you read. When you come to something that you consider amazing or surprising, exclaim, "Wow!" and write that fact inside the letter O.

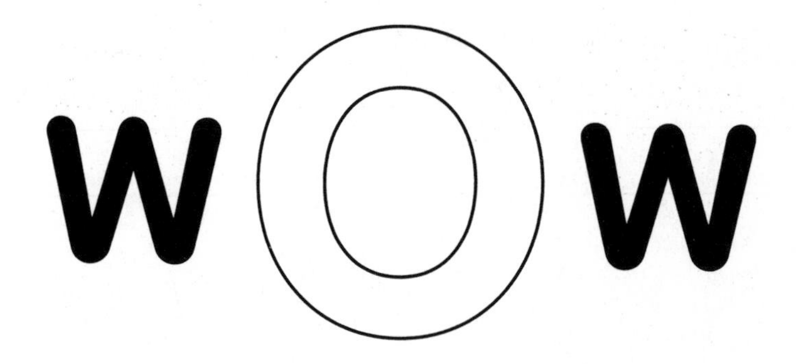

5. Distribute to students a sheet for recording their own "wow" discoveries. Instruct students to write *W-O-W* following your model. Have students read either an assigned or independent reading selection and challenge them to watch for and record "wow" discoveries. Be sure to remind them that because reading is very personal, you do not expect everyone to be surprised or amazed by the same things.

WHAT'S FACT, WHAT'S FANTASY?

Explanation

Young children quite often have difficulty separating reality from fantasy in text that they read. They tend naively to accept what's in print as truth. This lesson will raise their awareness and help them to recognize what's true and what's made up. The lesson provides an essential early step in developing critical thinking: no matter what their reading level, readers must always evaluate text and distinguish between fact and fiction. At the same time, the lesson is an opportunity for young readers to begin to recognize the different literary categories and to identify the genres of fiction and nonfiction.

Skill Focus

Distinguishing between fact and fantasy; distinguishing between fiction and nonfiction

Materials & Resources

Text

- One or more grade-appropriate fiction/fantasy book(s) and one or more nonfiction book(s): the subject matter of a selected fiction/fantasy book should be the same as that of a particular nonfiction book; all books should be clearly identifiable as fiction/fantasy or fact and should include illustrations (Used in this lesson: *Spiders* by Gail Gibbons and *The Itsy Bitsy Spider* by Lorianne Siomades)

Other

- For each student: 1 VIP strip with five fingers

Prior to the Lesson: *Before the start of this lesson, students should become familiar with the texts you'll use. You might read the books to the class during your regular read-aloud time or you might use books from previous guided reading lessons.*

STEPS

1. Explain to students that today they will be learning to understand the differences between two kinds of texts: fiction and fantasy books, which always tell made-up stories, and nonfiction books, which always present true information and facts. Display two books and share with students, "Remember when we read and enjoyed these books? Let's look at a couple of pages from each of them."

2. Focus first on the nonfiction book, holding that up for the class. For example, in the sample nonfiction book, you might turn to the page showing the crab spider. You might say something like, "This book is filled with interesting facts about real spiders that Gail Gibbons has researched. This book also uses detailed drawings to show us what the different spiders look like. Many informational books use photographs to illustrate information, but drawings like these can be just as helpful. When I realized that there were facts and real-life drawings of spiders in this book, I didn't get tricked by something else—the funny name that this spider has. It's a 'crab spider'! That sounds like something the author might have made up using her imagination, but all the other clues told me this was a true book so I know it is nonfiction."

3. Now hold up the selected fiction text. "Here's another book we read about spiders, *The Itsy Bitsy Spider* by Lorianne Siomades. Let's look at the cover. Just like the other book, this book uses drawings. But what do we see right away on the cover that tells us that this book isn't about something real?" Students should respond that the spider is wearing a sweater and rain boots and carrying an umbrella. Thumb to another illustration and ask students to describe it. Discuss the elements in the pictures that are imaginative and conclude by saying something like, "Boys and girls, we know that what we see on the pages of this book are things that we don't see in the real world. That means that this is fiction rather than fact."

4. Have students use VIP strips during independent or assigned text reading to mark elements that help them figure out whether the text is fact or fiction. They can put sticky notes on pictures and on the sentences that give them clues. At the end of the lesson, call on several students to share something they've marked with a sticky finger. Then, help to summarize why the text is fact or fantasy/fiction.

WHAT DID I JUST READ?

Explanation

Young readers often confuse "word calling" with reading. They can barrel right through a piece of text, calling words with great precision but not gaining any real meaning from what they've read. Having students stop, think, retell, and share as they read is a great strategy for helping them both develop and self-monitor comprehension.

Skill Focus

Retelling stories; recalling details in texts

Materials & Resources

Text

- Several examples of grade-appropriate, multi-paragraph fiction or nonfiction text that can be easily summarized in fewer words than the text itself (Used in this lesson: *Spiders* by Gail Gibbons)

Other

- Transparency or chalkboard

Bonus Ideas

Here's a follow-up strategy to use if students find they haven't understood the text and can't retell: Have them reread the text, making note of important words and thinking hard about how those words connect. Then they can try another retelling.

STEPS

1. Tell students that today they're going to learn a strategy that will help them remember more about the meaning of what they're reading. Write the words *STOP, THINK,* and *SHARE* on a transparency or on the board.

2. Read aloud a portion of your preselected text. Then say something like, "Now, I'll stop and think about what I've just read. Sometimes it helps to stop after reading only a short amount of text. Stopping lets me think about what I've read. I think about key words and ideas. Now I'm ready to retell what I've just read. When I retell and share what I read with someone, I use the key words to help put together all that I've learned. If I can tell about it clearly, there's a good chance that I understand it. And then I'll be able to continue reading." An example that demonstrates how the strategy works is below.

3. Distribute photocopies or display a transparency of another text selection. Challenge students to read it and practice the strategy of "Stop. Think. Share." You may want to set a timer and give them about five minutes to read. After the timer goes off, they are to stop and think silently for a few minutes. Now pair students and reset your timer. Within the allotted time, each partner should share what he or she thought the text said.

4. Have students conclude the discussion with their partners by telling whether or not they felt they understood the text.

Sample Text to Read Aloud	Stop and Think Aloud	Retell by Sharing Conversation
Spiders have a lot in common with each other, like eight legs, but there are many things that are different about them. They come in all different colors and in sizes from almost too tiny to see to many inches across. They live almost everywhere in the world in many different habitats. Spiders eat many things. Some eat other spiders, and some eat other insects like moths and crickets. Some even eat small animals.	"I'm remembering some important words from what I just read. I guess *spiders* would be the most important. I remember the word *different* and some key words that described the spiders' color, size, habitat, and what they eat. All of these words relate to spiders."	"I know that spiders all basically look the same. They have eight long legs that stick out from their body. But this article talked more about how spiders are different, and they really are different! They look different, live in many different places, and eat very different food—from other spiders to small animals. I'm thinking they're kind of like people. We have a lot in common but have lots of differences, too. I think I understood everything I just read."

HAVE WE MET BEFORE?

Explanation

One surefire sign that you've lost your understanding during reading is encountering an already introduced character whom you don't remember at all! This lesson will not only teach young readers that it's important to remember who the characters are and what their roles are in the text, but it will also provide them with a fun way of remembering those characters.

Skill Focus

Recognizing and remembering characters in text

Materials & Resources

Text

- Several narrative texts that each include two or more characters (Used in this lesson: *My Special Day at Third Street School* by Eve Bunting)

Other

- Transparency of the Character Outlines Organizer (see Appendix, page 117)
- For each student: a photocopy of the same organizer

Bonus Ideas

You can turn "Have We Met Before?" into a riddle game. Ahead of time, brainstorm characters, as well as their distinguishing qualities, from books the class has read during the year. Use this information to create riddles for students. For example, you might say, "I'm green and clever. I live in a garden. Have we met before?" (Answer: Philippe from *Philippe in Monet's Garden*)

STEPS

1. Tell students that all narrative texts have characters—some may be people, some animals, and some may even be "pretend" creatures (for example, aliens or inanimate objects that are personified). Explain that it's important for readers to remember each character once he, she, or it has been introduced in the text. Otherwise, the story might not make sense. Today you'll provide students with some good ways to get to know and remember a story's characters.

2. Using the overhead, display the transparency of the Character Outlines Organizer (Appendix, p. 117). Begin to read aloud a preselected story. When you encounter the first character, stop and write the name or description at the top of the figure that most closely represents that character (male outline for males, female outlines for females, animal outline for animals, and so on). For the sample text, your first step might be to write "the third-grade class" inside the group outline (since the class is preparing for the author's visit and no one single character stands out).

3. After naming a character on the outline, fill in the outline with key words or phrases that describe that character as you discover them. If you are using the example story, after naming the third-grade class, note the words *excited*, *eager*, and *getting ready* during your continued reading. When the author who visits the class is introduced, label the outline of a woman *Amanda Drake* and then jot down describing words like *an author, friendly, loves animals.*

4. Each time you re-encounter an already identified character, stop and comment something like, "Oh, I've already met that character. I remember that she's an author who's visiting the third-grade class. It helps me remember her because I already labeled an outline for her." Then add any new pertinent words to the outline. Note: If a story has more characters of one kind than there are shapes on the organizer, you might modify by drawing in several multiple small figures or creating one figure large enough to contain several names.

5. Distribute a photocopy of the Character Outlines Organizer to each student. Have students read a preselected narrative text selection and follow your model to take notes about the characters. Then read the story aloud (or have volunteers read it aloud). Each time you (or the student readers) come to a new character in the story, stop and say, "Who is this character? What words describe him/her?" Each time you come to an already identified character, stop and say, "Do you remember this character? Who is he/she?" Afterward, help students summarize why remembering characters in a story is so important to their understanding.

USING CONTEXT CLUES FOR UNDERSTANDING

Explanation

Young readers need to have readily available several quick strategies for figuring out unfamiliar words encountered during reading. Using context clues, especially in conjunction with the beginning sounds of words, is one such extremely helpful strategy. This lesson gives students a chance to practice that strategy in a game-like way that is also a lot of fun

Skill Focus

Figuring out unfamiliar words in text; using context clues to construct meaning

Materials & Resources

Text

- A large-font book or a Big Book, either fiction or nonfiction (Used in this lesson: *May I Go Out?* by Erin Rosenberg

Other

- 3″ x 3″ sticky notes
- Scissors

Bonus Ideas

Employ this strategy often with your texts, with sentences you make up using students' names, and with facts you've pulled from content you're studying. For example, you might choose key words like *snow* and *sleet* from a unit on weather. You could cover those two words in the sentence, "In cold climates, snow and sleet might fall," and discuss the different blends as you reveal the words.

***Prior to the Lesson:** Before the start of this lesson, read through the book you've chosen. Select about five or six words to mask out. Choose only words for which there is sufficient context (both syntactic and semantic) to allow students to make reasonable guesses about the word's identity. Place a sticky note, cut precisely to the size of the word, over each selected word. Next, make a snip with your scissors to create a flap in each sticky note. The flap should be cut so that, when lifted, it reveals only the beginning part of each word (all letters before the first vowel). At right is a diagram for the word* boots.

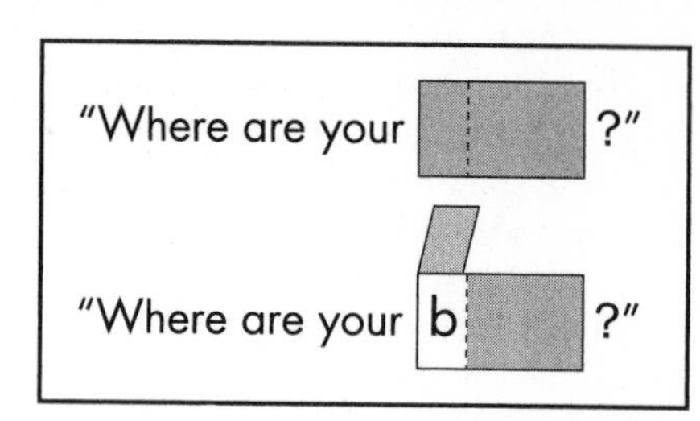

STEPS

1. Review with students how important it is to have available good strategies for dealing with words they don't immediately recognize when they're reading. They have to know how to figure them out in order to better understand what they're reading. Hold up the Big Book and introduce it to your class by explaining that during this read-aloud students are going to encounter words they can't immediately figure out. Read the book aloud, stopping when you come to words that are covered by the sticky notes. Say something like, "Oh, my! We have a mystery word here. Let's see if we can guess what's covered up!"

2. For each word, lead your students methodically through these steps to guess the word:

   - Read back over the sentence and ask, "What makes sense here?" Encourage students to focus on meaning in several ways. For instance, if a child suggests a singular word such as *coat*, demonstrate how *coat* couldn't fit in this sentence, but *gloves* could. Also, students should try to use the surrounding meaning of the story to suggest words. (If you have a chart or a board nearby, you might record their guesses. Stop with five or six.)

   - Pull back the flap to expose the initial part of the word (up to the first vowel). With students, eliminate the word choices that no longer work.

   - Tell students, "Shape your mouth to make the right sound for this letter(s)." Then ask, "What makes sense and starts this way?" (Have them volunteer additional reasonable guesses and add these to the list.)

   - Now pull off the sticky note completely to reveal the rest of the word. Encourage students to pay attention to all the letters in the word and to pronounce it. (If the word has already been listed, invite students to locate and confirm it on the list.)

Section Three

Generating and Answering Questions

From the moment good readers hold a book in their hands, they start to formulate questions. They ask themselves:

- What kind of book do I think this is?
- Have I read other books by this author?
- What were they about?
- Do I know anything about this topic?

And that's just the beginning—the pre-reading part. During reading, good readers are continually generating questions about the meaning of the text. In a fictional piece, they are wondering what a character will do next or how one plot twist will connect to another. In a nonfiction piece, they are assimilating facts that lead to unanticipated discoveries and further questions about those discoveries. It's an unending process, during which some questions are answered as others are formulated. And, often after the reading is done, unanswered questions remain. This simply means good readers have further inquiry, reading, and research ahead. In fact, a recurring series of questions and answers is what good reading is all about.

It follows, therefore, that instruction that focuses on questioning will improve students' reading. As the National Reading Panel reports: There is "strong empirical and scientific evidence that instruction of question generation during reading benefits reading comprehension in terms of memory and answering questions based on text as well as integrating and identifying main ideas through summarization" (2000).

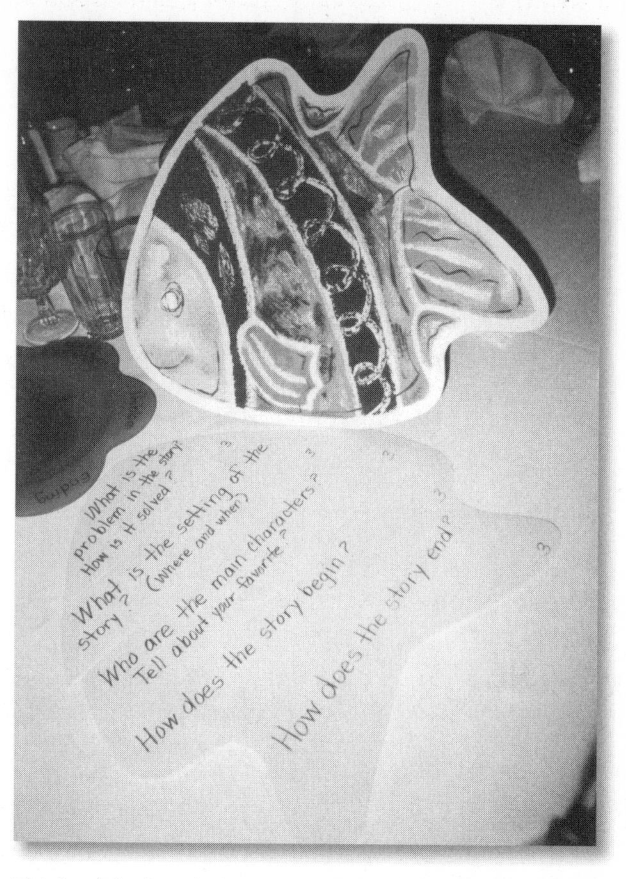

This fun fish-shaped placemat has been cut into puzzle pieces with basic comprehension questions on the back. As partners answer the questions, they put the story together—both literally and figuratively.

This section covers questioning from many different angles. One set of lessons takes children on an extended picture walk as they preview a book. Within a game-like framework based on the acronym *W-A-L-K*, they learn a system for asking and answering questions that is both deep and specific. During the "walk" they'll look for key words, author's purpose, and connections to their own lives and knowledge. And at the end of the walk, they'll learn to examine what they now know about the book so that they are fully prepared to sit down and read it.

In another series of lessons, students learn to judge whether a book is "just right" for them by asking five different questions. Each question helps them focus on a different aspect of the book—from word knowledge to fluency to level of thinking required—so that in the end they can successfully determine how well suited a particular book is for their own reading level. And in the process they are learning how to formulate excellent questions!

First graders are naturally curious. From the time they enter a classroom in the morning, they burst forth with a constant barrage of *Who? What? Why? When?* and *Where?* A good teacher can take that enthusiasm and curiosity and turn it to the child's great benefit in reading. It doesn't always make for a quiet, predictable classroom, but after all, we don't want them to be quiet, passive learners: encouraging the "noise" and the questions is part of the good teacher's job. Let's use their inquisitive nature as the catalyst for their becoming good readers! The lessons in this section should help you do just that. Have fun!

UNDER(THE)COVER DETECTIVES

Explanation

From the moment they spot a new book or selection, proficient readers automatically begin to make predictions about it. They formulate guesses about the text's likely genre, and they hypothesize about its contents, story line, difficulty level, and other elements. This lesson introduces students to the essential critical thinking/reading skill of making predictions in a whole-class and partner activity that resembles a guessing game.

Skill Focus

Using pictures and words to make and confirm predictions about stories; using text features/organizers (cover, title); asking and answering questions about texts

Materials & Resources

Text

- Two different texts (grade level or easier) with covers or beginning pages that include explicit picture and word clues about the contents (Big Books are excellent for this activity, although optional); you might consider using one text that's fiction and one that's nonfiction or informational for contrast

Bonus Ideas

To create a quick literacy center activity to follow up this lesson, place several books on a table, each with a rubber band wrapped around it so that it can't be opened. On the table, place a chart similar to the one on page 42. Invite students to use the chart to make notes about the books based on the cover illustrations and words.

STEPS

1. Display two books for the class. Tell students that they're going to be detectives today! Detectives look for clues that help them solve mysteries. The mystery today is—*What's inside these books?* Will students be able to tell what these books are about without actually reading them?

2. On the board, start a simple chart by listing the titles of the books. (See sample chart on page 42 for format.) Inform students that there are two types of clues that will be helpful to them in solving the mystery. Explain that one type of clue is a picture clue—clues provided by drawings, illustrations, and photographs. Write "Picture Clues" on the chart. Ask students to work with you to gather picture clues that can help them make predictions about what's in the books. Write their clues on the board.

3. The second type of clue your detectives will use is a word clue. Write "Word Clues" on the board chart and ask students to use the title and subtitle (if any) to note clues that might help them predict what they'll be reading about. List their comments.

4. After all clues are recorded, pair students and give them about two minutes to tell their buddy what they think each of the selections will be about. One partner can tell about one selection and one about the second selection. (You may want to help students with prompts such as: "Do you think it's a real or make-believe text?"; "Do you think it's funny or serious?"; "Do you think it'll give us good information?"; and "Will it tell a story?")

5. Gather the class together and add this phrase to your chart: "Because of the pictures and words, I think...." Call on different pairs to offer predictions they brainstormed. (It's all right to write predictions that you know are incorrect. All predictions will be either confirmed or corrected by the end of the lesson.)

6. After praising their keen detective skills, direct half of the class to read one selection and half to read the other. The purpose of their reading will be to report back to the whole class about how accurate the predictions have been.

7. After the reading, call on volunteers to place a checkmark next to the correct predictions and to cross out incorrect predictions. Discuss any differences in opinion with the class. Remember to praise even the incorrect predictions as good attempts so that students will continue to take risks in their prediction making.

Note: The chart below is provided to guide formatting and to illustrate the lesson's steps. You may also wish to use the two books highlighted here—unless you have already used them as suggested in the Section Two lesson on page 35. In that case, they will not work for predictions, because they will already be familiar to students.

	The Itsy Bitsy Spider **By Lorianne Siomades**	***Spiders*** **by Gail Gibbons**
Picture Clues	This is a drawing of a spider. The spider has a smile. The spider is wearing clothes and shoes. The spider is carrying an umbrella.	This is a drawing. The spider looks like a real one.
Word Clues	The words are funny–*itsy, bitsy.* The words rhyme.	This title isn't funny. The title is really focused–all it says is the word *spiders.* We recognize this author's name–she always writes books with good information.
Because of the pictures and words, I think...	This is a funny story. The book might rhyme since it has rhyming words on the cover. It's probably not about a real spider. It's probably not giving us information about spiders.	This will give us information about spiders. The information in this book will be true and factual.

FLIP: From Looking I Predict

Explanation

Young children are naturally curious about everything in the world around them. This lesson capitalizes on their tendency to ask questions and channels that into a good reading strategy. At the same time, it helps them recognize background knowledge they may already have about a topic—another key reading skill they'll need throughout their lives as readers.

Skill Focus

Using pictures and words to make and confirm predictions about stories; using text features/organizers (cover, title); asking and answering questions about texts; recognizing background knowledge

Materials & Resources

Text

- A grade-appropriate fiction or nonfiction reading selection that is unfamiliar to students; book should have a title and picture on the cover or beginning page that represents what the text is about (Used in this lesson: *Pancakes!* by J. Nayer)

Other

- 1 sheet of unlined paper
- Scissors
- For each student: 1 sheet of unlined paper

Steps

1. Tell students that today they're going to learn a fun technique for helping them make predictions about a book they're planning to read and for helping them recognize knowledge they already may have about the book's subject. They'll use both word and picture clues. Display the model book.

2. Hold up your sheet of paper and show students how you fold it in half lengthwise and then cut it so that it has three flaps. See diagram.

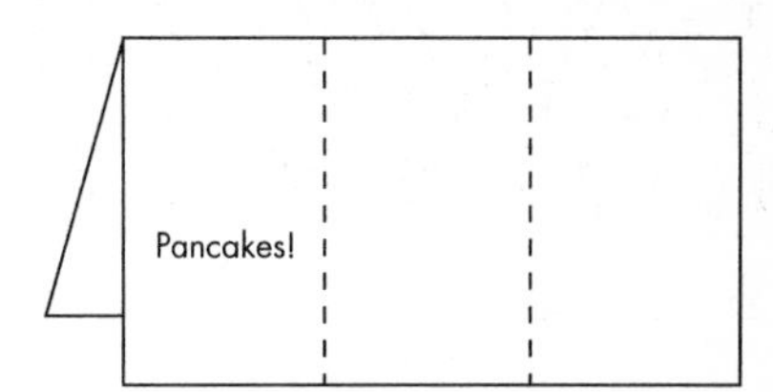

3. On the first flap, write the book's title. For example, with the book *Pancakes!* write just that one-word title. Open the flap. Make a prediction about what you'll be reading in this selection based on the title only—not the picture: "*Pancakes!* is a very simple title. I wonder if this book will give me information about how to make pancakes?" Write your prediction under the flap: "This book will tell me how to make pancakes."

4. On the middle outside flap, sketch something that replicates the cover or title-page picture. For this book, you might sketch a stick figure with its arms around several pancake shapes. Open the flap and explain that this is the place to write what the picture (not the words) makes you predict. For this book, you might explain that you have a different prediction based on the picture. You might say, "The picture doesn't make me think that this book will tell me how to make pancakes but will tell me about a boy who loves pancakes, because he's hugging a whole stack of them!" Write the sentence, "This book will be about a boy who loves pancakes."

5. On the third outside flap, sketch a figure that represents you—even a stick figure will do! Tell students that this is the place to write about or draw something that they already know about the book's topic. For example, with the model book, you might say something like, "I love to make pancakes. I make them for my kids on the weekends, and they love to help me stir the ingredients." Open the third flap and draw a bowl and a big spoon with several helping hands around the bowl.

6. Before students try this technique, remind them, "We should always make predictions before we read. We get our minds ready for what we think a selection will be about. We aren't always right, but it helps us as readers to make these guesses. We also think about what we already know about a subject. This helps us prepare to read, too. After I finish reading, I'm going to come back to my predictions to see which ones were right."

MINI-LESSON

TWO-PART LESSON: I'VE GOT A QUESTION

PART 1: RECORDING QUESTIONS

Explanation

Good readers constantly generate questions in their minds as they read. This means they are engaged with the text and actively thinking during reading. Sometimes they discover the answers on a subsequent page; sometimes they are still left wondering at the end of the selection. Either way, they are better readers because they are thinking about what they're reading. This lesson gives students a helpful procedure to get started with this strategy.

Skill Focus

Asking and answering questions about texts

Materials & Resources

Text

- A fiction or nonfiction reading selection of at least several pages (Note: nonfiction materials may elicit more questions for this activity)

Other

- Sticky notes in one color

Bonus Ideas

You might extend this into a math activity. Challenge students to create a bar graph to show how many of each question (*who, what, why, when,* and *where*) were written during the lesson. Have them graph each type and create a column for "other" as well.

STEPS

1. Explain to students that as good readers we ask ourselves lots of questions as we read. Sometimes the text answers those questions, but sometimes we don't know the answers even after we've read the whole book carefully. Reassure them that that's fine—often readers can get the information by rereading. And if that doesn't help and they still have questions, they can do a bit of further research.

2. Tell students that today you want them to share some of the good questions they think of as they read. Explain that there are two ways readers can remember their questions—often they will just hold them in their head, but sometimes they write them down as they go along. It helps to start by writing down the questions, which is what students will do today. On the board, write the title of the text you'll be reading, followed by headings for each page of the text. Use a format such as this:

   Title: ______________

   Page 1 Page 2 Page 3 Page 4

1. Read aloud page 1. Stop and think aloud about something you don't understand or that piques your curiosity. Write that question (keep it simple!) on a sticky note and place the note under the "Page 1" heading. Follow the same procedure for page 2.

2. For page 3, tell students you would like them to do the thinking and questioning. Read the page aloud to or with the class. Then ask if anyone has a question. Write each question on an individual sticky note and place all the notes under the page heading.

3. Continue in this manner for several subsequent text pages to make sure that students have had sufficient practice.

4. Sum up by reiterating that good readers ask themselves good questions the entire time they read. You might conclude by saying something like, "How many of you had a good question today while you read? That means you're on the way to being really great readers!" Building students' confidence as readers goes a long way! (Be sure to leave the sticky notes on the board for Part 2 of this lesson.)

Two-Part Lesson: I've Got a Question

Part 2: Rereading to Answer Questions

Explanation

Rereading text is an effective way for readers to answer the questions they have generated. This lesson helps students understand that we often get new information or understand something differently when we read a second and third time. This lesson extends the previous lesson so that students know what to do about unanswered questions. (Rereading is also an excellent way to help young readers develop fluency!)

Skill Focus

Asking and answering questions about texts; responding to texts through a variety of methods

Materials & Resources

Text

- Text used in Part 1 of this lesson

Other

- Sticky notes remaining on the board from Part 1 of this lesson
- Sticky notes of a different color from that used in Part 1

Bonus Ideas

Create a "Things We Wonder" bulletin board in your classroom. Every time an unanswered question arises from students' reading, add it to the bulletin board. Seeing their thoughtful questions recorded on the chart is a wonderful reward for good readers! (And, as a further bonus, you can use these questions as the basis for writing topics.)

Steps

1. Review with students what they learned in Part 1 of this lesson and introduce today's activity. You might say something like, "Yesterday we did what good readers do. We read each page of text and then stopped and asked ourselves questions about something we hoped to find out more about. We wrote our questions on sticky notes and placed them under the page number on the board. Today we're going to see how many of our questions are answered by the text."

2. Have students reread (either chorally, with partners, or independently) page 1 of the text used in Part 1. Tell them to stop at the end of that page.

3. Read aloud the question you had listed under the "Page 1" heading. Ask students if rereading this page has helped them answer this question. If so, write the answer (or have a student write it) on a different-colored sticky note and place it under the question. Follow the same procedure for page 2, with one additional step: have students consider whether the information on page 2 helps them answer the page 1 question and/or the page 2 question.

4. At this point, it's a good idea to remind students again that not all of a reader's questions are answered in the text. It's also helpful to encourage those students who may remember some answers to wait to answer until they've reached that portion of the text in the rereading.

5. Continue this process through the last page of the text. Review all the information that has been gathered on the sticky notes. Make a new column on the board titled "Things We Still Want to Know," and reposition to that column any sticky notes with questions that haven't yet been answered. Remind students that they might want to research the answers to these questions if they're really curious. (See Bonus Ideas for a follow-up activity.)

Four-Part Lesson: Picture Walk

Part 1: Starting the W-A-L-K: Words We Need to Know

Explanation

A picture walk is a tried-and-true activity for previewing texts, and there's a good reason for that—it works! With a little game-like twist, the method used in this four-part lesson allows students to become familiar with important vocabulary; to figure out the author's purpose; to activate prior knowledge by making connections; and to describe what they now know as they make predictions about the book. This first part of the lesson introduces students to the concept of the picture walk and focuses on key vocabulary.

Skill Focus

Asking and answering questions about texts; using pictures and words to make predictions about texts; identifying key words in text

Materials & Resources

Text

- A fiction or nonfiction Big Book with pictures that offer clear clues about text contents (Used in this lesson: *Growing Vegetable Soup* by Lois Ehlert)

Prior to the Lesson: *Before the start of the lesson, preview the book and decide which vocabulary words are critical for understanding the text. These are the words that you'll guide students to list during this part of the lesson. At this point, you might also jot down ideas to help you prepare for the subsequent three parts of the lesson: identifying author's purpose; establishing personal links with the text to activate prior knowledge; and recalling what a reader knows by now to make predictions about the book. (Note that the four underscored letters above spell W-A-L-K; these letters, in sequence, form a good framework for the four parts of this picture walk lesson and in fact for most of the important information that can be gathered during all of the picture walks you'll take.)*

Steps

1. Gather students around you. Write the letters *W-A-L-K* on the board, leaving a good bit of space between the letters. Explain that the four letters of this word are going to guide the class as you and they take a four-day walk. Instead of walking with your feet, though, you're all going to walk with your eyes and your minds. The walk will be through a new book!

2. Call attention to the book's cover. Invite the class to look and think with you as you model initial thoughts about and reactions to the book. Use sentence starters such as:

   "This reminds me of..."
   "I like books about..."
   "I wonder if this is about..."
   "This is a lot like..."
   "The picture makes me think..."

3. Using the same kinds of sentence starters, work your way through the book, turning pages slowly to stop and think aloud. You might occasionally ask students to tell you (or a buddy) what they're thinking on various pages. Note: If your selected book is especially long, you might skip some pages. Also, if the ending will be spoiled by previewing the pictures on the final page, you might choose not to highlight that page today.

4. Now focus students' attention on the four letters you wrote on the board. Point to the *W*. Tell students that this is the first letter of a word that describes an important thing you want them to remember from a picture walk. Challenge them to guess what the word that starts with *W* might be. Guide them as necessary to understand that when readers take a picture

walk through a book, they need to think about words that might be important in the text. Write Words under the *W* on the board.

5. Ask students to think about the pictures they saw and to help you list words they might expect to find in the text. What words might be important? List them under the *W*. A sample list for the text used in this lesson is below:

W	A	L	K
(Words) vegetables carrots rake seeds sun soil			

6. Remind students that good readers are constantly asking themselves questions as they read. Sometimes the questions, as in today's lesson, are about key words. But there are lots of other kinds of questions and they'll soon be taking other picture walks through this same book to ask some of these!

Bonus Ideas

Because even young children are motivated by earning money, you might occasionally follow up on this lesson by assigning dollar values to the words your students predict as they look at a book's title. Jot down their predictions on the board. Then, after reading, allow $1.00 for a word that was in the text and $2.00 for a word that was in the text and supported by a picture. (They'll love this even though they aren't getting real money!) It will likely get them to "pay" greater attention to their predictions. If you do this on a regular basis, you might keep a running total of how much money the class has earned. When they reach $100, they might earn a little surprise—free reading time, a popcorn snack, lunch in the courtyard, or something else that affirms that they are great predictors!

FOUR-PART LESSON: PICTURE WALK

PART 2: CONTINUING THE W-A-L-K: WHAT IS THE AUTHOR'S PURPOSE?

Explanation

A picture walk is a tried-and-true activity for previewing texts, and there's a good reason for that—it works! With a little game-like twist, the method used in this four-part lesson helps students become familiar with key aspects of a book. This second part of the lesson focuses on the author's purpose.

Skill Focus

Asking and answering questions about texts; using pictures and words to make predictions about texts; establishing purposes for reading

Materials & Resources

Text

- Same Big Book used in Part 1 (Used in this lesson: *Growing Vegetable Soup* by Lois Ehlert)

Other

- The word *W-A-L-K* and word list from Part 1, retained on chalkboard

STEPS

1. Ask students if they're ready to go on another picture walk today. Tell them they're going to be traveling the same path (that is, the same book) as yesterday, but they're going to be brainstorming for something else this time.

2. Start as you did in Part 1 by focusing on the cover and thinking aloud. However, this time vary the questions slightly and have students volunteer some of their own thinking about the cover. For example, you might ask them to think aloud about the following: "Does the picture on the front of the book remind you of anything else we've studied in class?" or "Do you think you'll like this book? Why or why not?"

3. Continue as in Part 1, turning the pages slowly and thinking aloud. Include some question variations, but it's fine to be a bit repetitive for this second day. This kind of repetition can be very helpful for many beginning readers. Just as you did in the first picture walk, occasionally ask students to tell you or a buddy what they're thinking on different pages.

4. Now it's time to reveal what the A stands for in the word *W-A-L-K*. Challenge students to guess what the word might be. Guide them as necessary to think about who an *author* is—the person who writes the text. Help them understand that authors always have a purpose or reason for writing. Sometimes they write to entertain us. Sometimes they write to give us some information. So, when readers take a picture walk through a book, they need to think about what the author's purpose was when he or she wrote that book. Under the A, write the words *Author's Purpose*.

5. Now ask students to think about the pictures in the book and to predict why they think the author wrote this text. Write their responses under the A. A sample list for the text used in this lesson is below:

W	A	L	K
(Words) vegetables carrots rake seeds sun soil	(Author's Purpose) inform us about vegetables teach us something about growing things		

FOUR-PART LESSON: PICTURE WALK

PART 3: CONTINUING THE W-A-L-K: WHAT LINKS DO YOU HAVE WITH THIS BOOK?

Explanation

With a little game-like twist, the method used in this four-part lesson helps students become familiar with key aspects of a book. In this third part, students make connections between their own life experiences and a text in order to activate prior knowledge.

Skill Focus

Asking and answering questions about texts; using pictures and words to make predictions about texts; establishing purposes for reading; making connections between texts and prior knowledge, other texts, and the world

Materials & Resources

Text

- Same Big Book used in Parts 1 and 2 (Used in this lesson: *Growing Vegetable Soup* by Lois Ehlert)

Other

- The word *W-A-L-K* and word lists from Parts 1 and 2, retained on chalkboard

Bonus Ideas

Give a narrow paper strip to each student. Instead of having students share their connections to the topic aloud, have them write their connections on the strips. Use a stapler or tape to connect all the strips as chain links. Hang this on the board and brag about how well your students make links with the texts they're reading!

STEPS

1. Tell students that today is their third chance to go on a picture walk. Share that in this lesson they're going to find out what the *L* stands for in the word *W-A-L-K*. Explain that since you've all spent a good bit of time walking through the pages of this book, today you'll take a quick flip—a quick trip!—through the book. Invite them to get their eyes and minds ready to walk.

2. After flipping through all pages of the book with the class, call attention again to the word *W-A-L-K* written on the board. Review the significance of the first two letters that have been revealed—*Words* and *Author's Purpose*.

3. Now ask if students have come up with any possible suggestions for the letter *L*. Discuss students' ideas. This is a tricky one to guess so it's likely that you'll need to explain that the *L* word is *Links*. Write *Links* under the *L* on the board. Explain that links connect things. Give students some simple examples of links. For example, some buildings have walkways that link them to other buildings. Chains have lots of links that connect them to one another. You might also use sketches on the board to help illustrate the concept of a link. Explain that we can better understand what we read when we can link it to things that we already know or to experiences we've had in our own lives.

4. Ask students if the pictures they've previewed remind them of any experiences or things they know. Model your own links to the book to help students get started. A sample list for the text used in this lesson is shown below, as added to the ongoing *W-A-L-K* chart on the board:

W	A	L	K
(Words) vegetables carrots rake seeds sun soil	(Author's Purpose) inform us about vegetables teach us something about growing things	(Links) My parents have a garden. We have some of the same tools in our garden. I have raked our yard with my dad.	

FOUR-PART LESSON: PICTURE WALK

PART 4: CONCLUDING THE W-A-L-K: WHAT DO YOU KNOW NOW ABOUT THIS BOOK?

Explanation

After three previous walks through a book, students now benefit from one last pass. In this final part of the lesson, students recall what they feel they've learned from the picture walk. As they describe what they feel they know by now, they are really making predictions about the text they're about to read—a key reading skill they've learned while they've been having fun!

Skill Focus

Asking and answering questions about texts; using pictures and words to make predictions about texts; recalling details in texts

Materials & Resources

Text

- Same Big Book used in Parts 1, 2, and 3 (Used in this lesson: *Growing Vegetable Soup* by Lois Ehlert)

Other

- The word *W-A-L-K* and word lists from Parts 1, 2, and 3, retained on chalkboard

STEPS

1. Ask students if they're ready to go on one last picture walk through the same book they've already journeyed through several times. Share that today they're going to find out what the last letter—*K*—stands for in the word *W-A-L-K*. Tell them to get their eyes and minds ready to walk once more!

2. For this final walk, you might have one or more students help you turn the pages. Go through the book quickly, as you did in Part 3.

3. Call attention again to the word *W-A-L-K* written on the board. Review the significance of the first three letters that have been revealed—*Words*, *Author's Purpose*, and *Links*.

4. Now reveal that the *K* in *W-A-L-K* stands for *Know*. Write *Know* under the *K* on the board. Say something like, "We've already spent a good deal of time previewing this book. Now is the time to think about what we know from doing our picture walk. This will help us predict what this book is all about." Conclude by asking, "So, what do you think you *know* about what we'll be reading in this book?" List students' responses under the *K* on the board. A sample list for the text used in this lesson is shown below, as added to the ongoing *W-A-L-K* chart on the board:

W	A	L	K
(Words) vegetables carrots rake seeds sun soil	(Author's Purpose) inform us about vegetables teach us something about growing things	(Links) My parents have a garden. We have some of the same tools in our garden. I have raked our yard with my dad.	(Know) The book is about growing vegetables. It's about how seeds grow. It's about what plants need to grow. There are many kinds of vegetables.

5. Praise students' efforts—this has been a long (but hopefully interesting) walk! Now, every time you do a picture walk, you can have students go through the *W-A-L-K* questions for a great preview of what's to come.

SHAPING QUESTIONS

Explanation

Students need to learn to write good questions about text they've read. This lesson provides instruction about the nature and characteristics of good questions, while allowing students to have fun writing their questions on special shapes. And, if you choose to use the Bonus Idea, you'll also wind up with a great bulletin board to stimulate thinking about text and content studied in your class.

Skill Focus

Asking and answering questions about texts

Materials & Resources

Text

- Nonfiction text, several pages in length, that provides good basis for student questions (Used in this lesson: *Bugs! Bugs! Bugs!* by Jennifer Dussling)

Other

- Die shapes and die-cut machine
- Special die-cut figures that correspond to the theme of your reading selection (for sample lesson, figures are cut into bug shapes)
- Construction paper

Bonus Ideas

After the lesson, pin the shapes on a bulletin board and encourage students to visit the board to review what was learned in the text, to learn new things, and for some great writing topics!

Prior to the Lesson: *Use your school's die-cut machine to prepare the figures that students will use in this lesson. For each figure, fold a piece of construction paper in half lengthwise or widthwise to fit the die. (You may be able to get more than one shape per sheet of paper.) Place the paper under the die cutter, positioning the folded edge just inside the blade at a spot that will form a nice hinge. Once you cut the die, you should have two figures with a hinged edge as shown in the diagram at right.*

STEPS

1. Review with students the characteristics of good questions. Start a list on the board that includes these key points:
   - Good questions need to express a complete thought and make sense.
   - Good questions need to include question words.
2. Continue by having students brainstorm a list of question words. Add their responses to the list started in Step 1. Guide them to include the words *who, what, when, where, why, how much*, and *how many*.
3. Read aloud a brief section of your sample text to give students a sense of the topic. Ask them, "What kinds of things would someone want to know about what I just read aloud? Let's see how many different questions we can make up about the text I read." Below is an example of possible questions based on the sample text:
   - How does a praying mantis catch its food?
   - How can ants carry something so much larger than they are?
4. Tell students that they will now finish reading the text independently. Their job is to think of a good question as they read. They will record this question in a special way after reading. While students read, circulate around the room, providing support as needed.
5. Review with students the additional characteristics that apply to written questions. Elicit the points below and add them to the list on the board:
   - Good questions need to start with a capital letter.
   - Good questions need to end with correct punctuation—a question mark.
6. Distribute to each student a prepared die-cut shape. On the outside of the shape, they are to write the question they have thought of. On the inside, they are to write the answer to the question (if they feel they know it).
7. Conclude by having a few students quiz the class with their questions. If no one gets the answer correct, encourage class discussion.

FIVE-PART LESSON: IS THIS A JUST-RIGHT BOOK?

PART 1: DO I KNOW ANYTHING ABOUT THIS TOPIC?

Explanation

Too often, students wind up reading with little comprehension because there is a mismatch between the text and the reader's ability to read and understand that text. Thus, one of the most important questions a reader can learn to ask is, "Is this book right for me?" There are five ways to discover the answer. This lesson introduces the concept of finding a just-right book and explores the first means of answering the question.

Skill Focus

Asking and answering questions about texts; using pictures and words to make predictions about texts; using simple text features to obtain information

Materials & Resources

Text

- A fiction or nonfiction book, with a title and cover that clearly define the topic (Used in this lesson: *Philippe in Monet's Garden* by Lisa Jobe Carmack)
- Regular assigned reading book(s) and/or classroom library and school library books

Other

- Poster board
- Marker

Bonus Ideas

This lesson series' poster can be displayed throughout the year as a resource for students as they make book selections.

Note: *Although these lessons walk your students through the five separate questions in a step-by-step manner, it's important to realize that over time, the questions will become so familiar to students that you'll be able to ask several—and eventually all five—at once. Thus, what might appear like a long and even repetitive process here will ultimately be quick and internalized, enabling students to make independent choices.*

STEPS

1. Explain to students that choosing the right books to read is very important. Sometimes a book might look like fun but it's so simple that it's boring. Other times, a book might turn out to be way too difficult to understand. So figuring out ahead of time whether a book is "just right" is really important. Explain that today and for the next four days, you're going to show the class a great technique for asking questions that will help them know if a book is right for them. And since you're a reader and this technique works for all readers, you're going to show them what you do yourself to get them started.

2. Write this title on the poster board: "Is This a Just-Right Book?" Say something like, "When I choose a book to read at the library or at the bookstore, here's the first question I ask myself to see if it's just right for me." Write this question on the chart: "Do I know anything about this topic?"

3. Next explain, "I can probably tell if I already know something about a book from looking at the cover and reading the title. I'll stop to ask myself, 'What do I already know about this?' If I don't know anything about the topic, I figure the book will probably be a little harder for me to read. Even so, I might try it if I really want to learn something new. But it's good for me to know that ahead of time so I can be more aware of my comprehension as I read."

4. Model the process you described in Step 3. Display a book, look at the cover, and read aloud the topic. Think aloud about a few things you know about the topic. For example, with the sample book, *Philippe in Monet's Garden*, you might share, "I know that there was a very famous artist named Monet who lived long ago in France. He had a beautiful garden, and his paintings of his garden are also very famous. I wonder if this book has something to do with that artist?"

5. Have students preview book titles and covers by looking through their assigned reading book(s) at different selections or by checking through books in the classroom and/or school library. Tell them to ask themselves the question, "What do I know about this topic?" Have them discuss their discoveries and reactions with a partner or in a whole-class discussion.

FIVE-PART LESSON: IS THIS A JUST-RIGHT BOOK?

PART 2: DO I UNDERSTAND WHAT I'M READING?

Explanation

Too often, students wind up reading with little or no comprehension because there is a mismatch between the text and the reader's ability to read and understand that text. In this second measure of a book's suitability, readers monitor initial comprehension to decide if they understand the material.

Skill Focus

Monitoring comprehension; asking and answering questions about texts; retelling stories; recalling details in text

Materials & Resources

Text

- A grade-appropriate fiction or nonfiction book (Used in this lesson: *Philippe in Monet's Garden* by Lisa Jobe Carmack)
- A preselected assortment of grade-appropriate books and/or the books in your regular classroom library

Other

- Poster board with list started in Part 1; marker

Bonus Ideas

Introduce students to some classical art—Auguste Rodin's bronze sculpture, *The Thinker.* Stress that smart readers think really hard just like the man in this famous sculpture. You might even suggest that they strike this "fist to the chin" pose as they think about their reading!

STEPS

1. Point to the poster-board chart you began during Part 1 of this lesson. Briefly review the concept of finding just-right books and the first question on the chart, which was the focus of the previous lesson.

2. Add this second question to the chart: "Do I understand what I'm reading?" Tell students, "As good readers, we read a little of the book we're thinking about reading to see if it's something we'll understand. While we read, we constantly ask ourselves if we understand everything we read. We might stop and summarize what we've just read or retell it to ourselves." Let students know they don't have to read much of the book to judge whether they're able to understand it—a few paragraphs or the first page is usually enough.

3. Hold up your selected text and open it to the beginning page. Model how you read the beginning sentences or paragraph(s). Stop and retell a bit, "Now let me stop and see if I understand what I've read." For example, with the sample book, you might read the first two pages and then think aloud, "Hmm . . . I'm not sure if this book will have anything to do with the famous artist I know about, but it does take place in France where the artist Monet lived. Here's what I've learned so far: There's a frog named Philippe who has really big feet and who takes really big leaps. But there seems to be a problem for him—his friends treat him unkindly."

4. After your retelling, say something like, "I'm thinking about what I just read and I can tell that the meaning makes sense to me. So, I think this is going to be a just-right book for me!"

5. Now call attention to the assortment of books you've set up and/or to your classroom library. Invite students to select a book and to read its beginning, just as you have modeled. Announce a time limit of four minutes. Organize the class into partners. Have students describe to their partner what they've just read and whether they think the book is just right for them.

FIVE-PART LESSON: IS THIS A JUST-RIGHT BOOK?

PART 3: DO I KNOW MOST OF THE WORDS?

Explanation

Too often, students wind up reading with little or no comprehension because there is a mismatch between the text and the reader's ability to read and understand that text. This lesson focuses on the third measure of the five by allowing readers to assess whether enough vocabulary in a reading selection is familiar.

Skill Focus

Asking and answering questions about texts; using pictures and words to make predictions about texts; drawing conclusions

Materials & Resources

Text

- A grade-appropriate fiction or nonfiction book (Used in this lesson: *Philippe in Monet's Garden* by Lisa Jobe Carmack)
- A fiction or nonfiction book that is too difficult for most of your students (Used in this lesson: *The Hoboken Chicken Emergency* by Daniel Pinkwater)
- A pre-selected assortment of both grade-appropriate books and above-grade-level books

Other

- Poster board with ongoing list from Parts 1 and 2
- Marker

STEPS

1. Review the two questions previously written on the chart and briefly discuss how and why they are important in choosing a just-right book. Then reveal the third question as you add it to the chart: "Do I know most of the words?"

2. Tell students that a book can be just right for them even if it has a few new words. That's how we all grow as readers and learn new vocabulary. However, if a book has too many difficult words for a reader, he or she will not be able to read the book comfortably nor truly understand it.

3. Display a fairly difficult book and attempt to read the first paragraph(s) or page. Model how you struggle with several words. (Be sure to tell students that you're role-playing being a first grader!) For example, with the sample difficult book, *The Hoboken Chicken Emergency*, you might exclaim, "I'm confused about what I've just read. I couldn't figure out how to read those words I stumbled over—*suspected*, *holiday*, *celebrate*, *ungrateful*, *Poland*, and *arguing*. Overall, I think there were too many unfamiliar words for me. This wouldn't be a just-right book for me. I need to keep looking for one that I'll understand and enjoy."

4. Now model reading the beginning sentences or paragraph(s) of the sample appropriate book. (Explain that you'll read it as though you're a first grader; this will allow you to miss a word or two.) Stop and report, "Now let me think how many words are new words or tough words for me to figure out. If I were in first grade, the words *countryside* and *marvelous* would be really big and tough for me. But, I think if I don't have more than a tough word or two on a page, and if I still understand what it's saying, then this is a just-right book for me."

5. Now call attention to the assortment of books you've set up, and invite students to select several books each. Have students read the beginning page of each book and retell (to you or a partner) what they remember. After the retelling, the reader should count on his or her hands how many words were too difficult to read. One or two fingers means the book is probably a just-right book; three or more fingers means it is probably too difficult.

PART 4: ARE THERE ONLY A FEW PLACES WHERE MY READING IS CHOPPY?

Explanation

Too often, students wind up reading with little or no comprehension because there is a mismatch between the text and the reader's ability to read and understand that text. This lesson focuses on the fourth of the five measures used to answer that question by challenging readers to assess whether their reading of a particular book is fluent or too choppy.

Skill Focus

Monitoring comprehension; asking and answering questions about texts

Materials & Resources

Text

- A grade-appropriate fiction or nonfiction book (Used in this lesson: *Philippe in Monet's Garden* by Lisa Jobe Carmack)
- A fiction or nonfiction book that is too difficult for most of your students (Used in this lesson: *The Boxcar Children* by Gertrude Chandler Warner)
- A preselected assortment of both grade-appropriate books and above-grade-level books

Other

- Poster board with ongoing list from Parts 1, 2, and 3
- Marker

STEPS

1. Review the previous three questions you've listed on the chart, and briefly discuss how and why they are important in choosing a just-right book. Then reveal the fourth question as you add it to the list: "Are there only a few places where my reading is choppy?"

2. Tell students that one of the goals of a good reader is to read the print without having it sound choppy. Say something like, "We want to read the text smoothly—almost the way we talk in our 'everyday lives.' "

3. Display a fairly difficult book and attempt to read the first paragraph(s) or page. Model reading with a choppy cadence, pausing between words, repeating words, and mispronouncing a few words. (Again, be sure to tell students that you're role-playing being a first grader!) Conclude your reading by thinking aloud, "I can't remember much about what I just read. I guess I was concentrating so hard on the difficult words and sentences that I didn't understand the text. Let me keep looking for a just-right book."

4. Now model how you read the first two pages of the sample appropriate book, *Philippe in Monet's Garden*, with fluency—good phrasing and a natural cadence (even though you might model stumbling over a word or two). Announce to your students, "I can understand everything I've just read. This would be a just-right book for me!"

5. Call attention to the assortment of books you've set up, and invite students to each select several books. Have students read the beginning page of each book. Challenge them to decide whether they read the book with a smooth or a choppy voice. Circulate about the room as they read, offering guidance and advice as appropriate. Conclude the lesson by having a few volunteers share their experiences.

FIVE-PART LESSON: IS THIS A JUST-RIGHT BOOK?

PART 5: DO I THINK WHILE I'M READING THIS BOOK?

Explanation

In this final lesson in the series, students will experience books that are too simple as well as books that are too difficult. (It's important for even beginning readers to realize that a book that doesn't make them think is too simple for them.) By making comparisons with text at either end of the spectrum, they can more clearly understand what makes a book just right. It's almost like a "Goldilocks and the Three Bears" experiment: a search to find the book that is just the right "size" and well suited to the reader!

Skill Focus

Monitoring comprehension; asking and answering questions about texts

Materials & Resources

Text

- A pre-first-grade, predictable book (Used in this lesson: *Five Little Monkeys* by E. Christelow)
- A grade-appropriate fiction or nonfiction book (Used in this lesson: *Philippe in Monet's Garden* by Lisa Jobe Carmack)
- An above-grade-level fiction or nonfiction book (Used in this lesson: *Amazing Buildings* by Kate Hayden)
- A preselected, randomly mixed assortment of grade-appropriate, below-grade-level, and above-grade-level books

Other

- Poster board with list from Parts 1, 2, 3, and 4; marker

STEPS

1. Review the four questions previously written on the chart and briefly discuss how and why they are important in choosing a just-right book. Then add the fifth and final question to the chart—"Do I think while I'm reading this book?"

2. Tell students that good readers need to be active thinkers while they read. Say something like, "If I'm reading without even having to think, the book is much too easy. A just-right book will make me think. In fact, reading is all about thinking! But, if I have to think too much, I probably won't enjoy the book and it won't be right for me. So there's a balance that I'm looking for."

3. Open to the beginning page of the easy book. Model reading the beginning with total fluency. For example, with the sample easy book, *Five Little Monkeys*, you might stop and report, "Now that was so easy for me. I really didn't have to stop and think about it to understand it. I used to jump rope as I sang this song. So, I already knew most of the words without reading! Let me find something that's more challenging."

4. Hold up the difficult book you've selected. Tell students you'll read it as if you were a first grader. Stop after every sentence or two to say, "Let me see—what have I just read?" Model struggling to make sense of the book. With the sample difficult book, *Amazing Buildings*, you might say, "Goodness! This book has some great pictures, but the words are pretty hard—*ancient*, *Colosseum*, *gladiators*, and *echoes*. I have to think too hard with this book! Let me see if I can find something else that might be a just-right book that I can enjoy reading. I'll come back to this book later when I've had more reading practice."

5. Next, read an excerpt from a grade-appropriate text. Read it with fluency, hesitating only occasionally. For example, for the sample book you might say, "I have to think because there are a few new words and there are also some new things that I'm learning. There are some rhyming words that help me, too." Then exclaim, "Yes, this is a just-right book for me!"

6. Now call attention to the assortment of books you've set up and invite students to each select several books. Have students read the beginning page of each book within a time limit of three to four minutes. When time is up, have students stop and discuss either as a whole group or with a partner whether the book they sampled made them think too little, too much, or "just right"!

Section Four

Using Graphic and Semantic Organizers

Graphic and semantic organizers—diagrams or pictorial representations that visually illustrate concepts and relationships—play an essential role in building students' reading comprehension. Adaptable for use with just about any kind of fiction or nonfiction text, they make vague and abstract ideas concrete so that students can more easily process and understand these concepts.

The National Reading Panel reports that these tools have a positive impact on three specific areas of learning:

1. They help students focus on text structure while reading.

2. They provide a framework that visually represents textual relationships.

3. They facilitate students' writing well-organized summaries. (NRPR, 2000)

The National Reading Panel research also says that "teaching students to use a systematic, visual graphic to organize the ideas that they are reading about develops the ability of the students to remember what they read and may transfer in general to better comprehension and achievement in social studies and science content areas." (NRPR, pp. 4–75)

For this author, and others in past generations, the closest experience to using true graphic organizers was the venerable exercise of diagramming sentences. The sentence diagram (which offered a means of picturing the technical aspects of sentence construction) can even be seen as a precursor to today's graphic organizers. Many students may have huffed and grunted, "Why are we doing this?" but in the end, relationships among sentence parts were distilled and represented in a uniquely clear way. Some of us may hate to admit it, but we actually enjoyed this puzzle of lines! We are not advocating going back to sentence-diagramming days, but realizing the strengths of this approach can help us better grasp the valuable role of all graphics in literacy instruction. Indeed, such graphics can be the key for some students—especially those who are visual learners—in achieving comprehension of many abstract concepts.

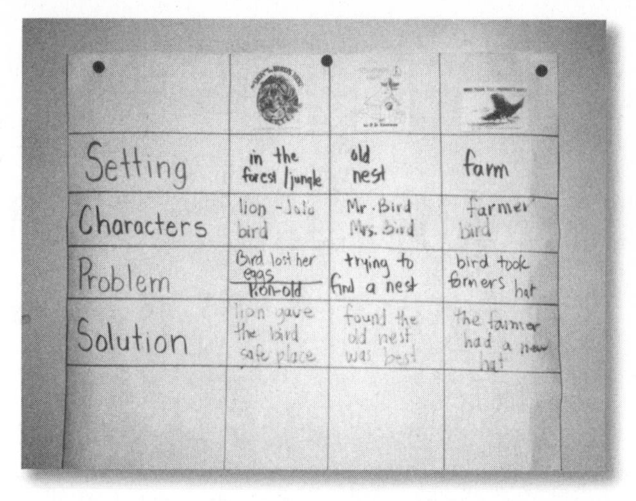

This chart demonstrates how one class has compared the narrative elements in three different texts.

Here is one teacher's creative version of a Story Hand—she's labeled and decorated the outer side of the glove in her own unique way!

Although there are countless versions of organizers available, the research of Bromley, Irwin-De Vitis, and Modlo (1995) suggests that there are four basic structures from which all graphic and semantic organizers evolve: conceptual, sequential, hierarchical, and cyclical. In the lessons in this section, you will find examples of all four structures. Because you're working with first graders, however, many of the concept maps in these lessons have an additional angle: they've been made more kinesthetic and tactile. For example, students are asked to physically hold an organizer's text ovals and arrows or to act out the relationships these tools embody. In this way, we hope to address both the early developmental stages and the different learning styles of your children.

Have fun with your students as you engage in learning through graphic and semantic organizers!

FIVE-PART LESSON: GIVE THE STORY A HAND

PART 1: CHARACTER

Explanation

Beginning readers need to learn about the five basic story elements as they delve further into fiction reading. Learning about the elements through this unique 3-D graphic organizer will really make an impression on them. Most graphic organizers are one-dimensional diagrams on paper, but this one is tactile and can be touched and held, providing a further means of reinforcing students' new knowledge. In this first lesson of five, you create the basic Story Hand and then focus on the element of characters.

Skill Focus

Using graphic/semantic organizers to organize information; identifying story elements (characters)

Materials & Resources

Text

- A narrative text with clear story elements

Other

- A plain canvas gardening glove
- Permanent markers in a variety of colors
- Story Hand Buttons template, optional but highly suggested for English-language learners (Appendix, p. 118)
- Glue

STEPS

1. Explain to students that just about all stories share five elements, or characteristics, in common. The five elements are characters, setting, plot, problem, and solution. It's important for readers to be aware of these elements because understanding how a story is built helps deepen their comprehension. By knowing the elements to look for, readers have a framework for understanding a story.

2. Tell students that in order to help them picture and remember these five elements, you're going to create something new for the classroom. In this and the next four lessons, you will turn an ordinary gardening glove into a special Story Hand that you will keep on display in the classroom for the rest of the year to remind the class of how stories are built.

3. Gather the class around you and hold up the glove. Start by decorating the outer side. You might draw the outline of fingernails with a black marker, add lines for knuckles, and draw a ring on one of the fingers. You might even paint the nails a color (unless you think that won't be well received by the boys!). Let your creativity flow. (See page 58 for one teacher's unique Story Hand.)

4. Now turn the glove to the inner, palm side. On one of the fingers write the word *character*. If you're using the Story Hand Buttons template (Appendix, p. 118), hot-glue the appropriate "button" to the fingertip.

5. Point to the labeled finger and tell students that characters is one of the five elements. You might say something like, "Stories always have characters. Sometimes the characters are people, but sometimes they are animals. Sometimes they're realistic and sometimes they're imaginative. Sometimes authors even treat items like trees or cars like they're characters. That's kind of tricky, so we'll have to watch for that!"

6. Extend the discussion by pointing out that television shows, movies, and cartoons have characters, too. You might brainstorm some of those familiar to your students. List them on the board, creating one column for the story or show and another for the characters.

7. Finally, read aloud a simple story. With students, decide who the characters are. Also, decide who the main character is—the one that the story is mainly about. Conclude by pinning the Story Hand to a bulletin board and piquing students' interest about what the next finger/element might be.

FIVE-PART LESSON: GIVE THE STORY A HAND

PART 2: SETTING

Explanation

Learning about the five basic story elements through this unique 3-D graphic organizer will really make an impression on students. The five lessons don't necessarily need to be taught consecutively. You may wish to space them out a bit to give students practice with each element using different approaches. This lesson teaches students to identify setting as an important story element.

Skill Focus

Using graphic/semantic organizers to organize information; identifying story elements (setting)

Materials & Resources

Text

- A narrative text with clear story elements

Other

- The gardening glove used in Part 1
- Permanent markers in a variety of colors; glue
- Story Hand Buttons template, optional but highly suggested for English-language learners (Appendix, p. 118)

Bonus Ideas

To help students with their own story writing, create a poster illustrating different times and places and display it in your class writing center. Alert students that they might find a perfect setting for their story there.

STEPS

1. Tell students you think they're ready to learn something else about how stories are made. Hold up the Story Hand from Part 1 and, in a different-colored marker from the one used to write *character*, add the word *setting* to a second finger. If you're using the Story Hand Buttons template (Appendix, p. 118), glue the appropriate "button" to the setting fingertip.

2. Share with students that setting is where and when a story happens. On the board, write "Places We Know." Tell students that *where* refers to a place in which something happens. Invite them to help you brainstorm a list of places. Here is a sample brainstormed list:

   Places We Know

school	forest	bedroom	beach
home	restaurant	theater	mountains
library	street	New York	garden

3. Write "Times We Know" on the board and brainstorm a new list for different words that describe "when" a story might take place. Encourage and guide students as necessary to think of as many time-related words as possible. Here is a sample list:

   Times We Know

morning	afternoon	night	summer
winter	spring	fall	years
today	yesterday	hours	minutes

4. Finally, read aloud a simple story. Together with your students decide what the setting is. Challenge them to find words in the story that are clues to the setting.

FIVE-PART LESSON: GIVE THE STORY A HAND

PART 3: PLOT

Explanation

What's a story without a plot? This lesson, the third in this group of lessons, teaches students to recognize a story's plot. In the lesson, you continue to create a unique 3-D graphic organizer for students by adding the third finger to the Story Hand.

Skill Focus

Using graphic/semantic organizers to organize information; identifying story elements (plot); retelling stories

Materials & Resources

Text

- A narrative text with clear story elements

Other

- The gardening glove used in Parts 1 and 2
- Permanent markers in a variety of colors; glue
- Story Hand Buttons template, optional but highly suggested for English-language learners (Appendix, p. 118)

Bonus Ideas

Once the glove is complete, use it to help students distinguish between narrative text and other genres. Have small groups identify narrative texts from a random assortment of books. As groups present their selections to the class, one group member can wear the glove.

STEPS

1. Tell students that today they'll learn about a third key story-building block, or element. Hold up the Story Hand from Parts 1 and 2 and, in a different-colored marker from those used previously, add the word *plot* to a third finger. If you're using the Story Hand Buttons template (Appendix, p. 118), glue the appropriate "button" to the plot fingertip.

2. Discuss with students that *plot* is the word we use for the action and the events—that is, everything that happens—in a story. The plot happens in steps—something happens first, then another event occurs, then another, and so on. Draw an outline of a staircase of steps on the board.

3. Have students recall a familiar fairy tale, such as "Cinderella" or "Hansel and Gretel." Start a plot summary by writing the first two major events on the bottom two steps. Then invite students to help you retell the other major story events. Write them in order on the remaining steps.
   For "Cinderella," the steps might look like this:

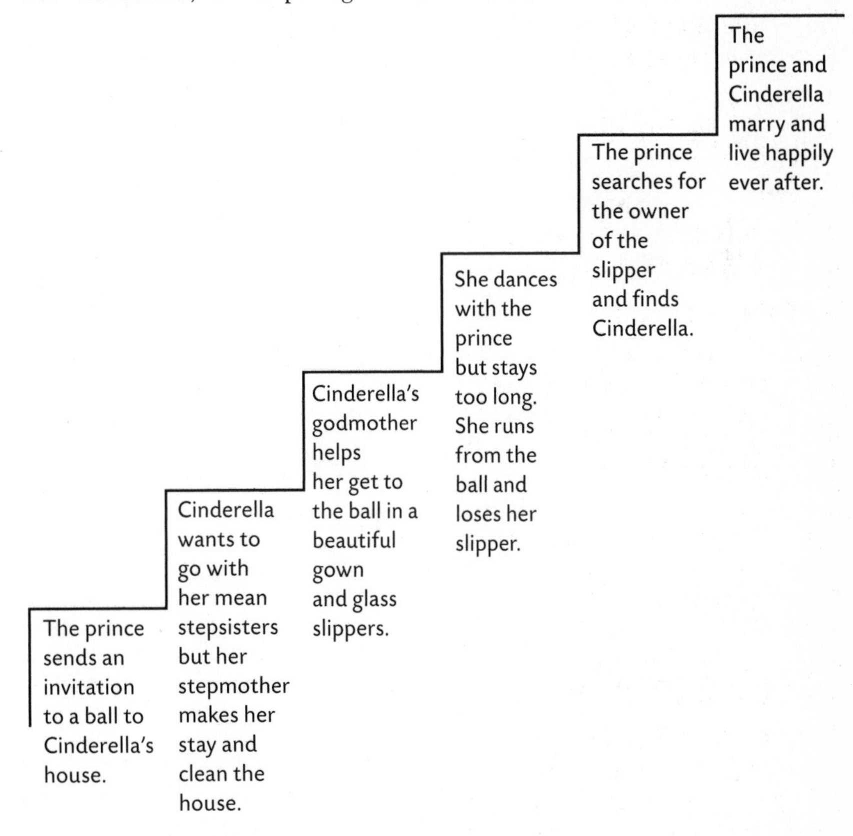

4. Finally, read aloud a simple story. Together with your students, retell the story, writing the events on steps just as you did for the fairy tale.

FIVE-PART LESSON: GIVE THE STORY A HAND

PART 4: PROBLEM

Explanation

This lesson, the fourth in this group of lessons about the basic story elements, teaches students that almost all narratives revolve around conflicts. This lesson helps students connect to that concept through personal experiences.

Skill Focus

Using graphic/semantic organizers to organize information; identifying story elements (problem); recalling details in text

Materials & Resources

Text

- A narrative text with clear story elements

Other

- The gardening glove used in Parts 1, 2, and 3
- Permanent markers in a variety of colors; glue
- Story Hand Buttons template, optional but highly suggested for English-language learners (Appendix, p. 118)
- 3 transparencies

Bonus Ideas

During students' reading conferences with you, use your completed Story Hand as a way to stimulate discussion. Give students the glove to wear and let them discuss one of the elements as it relates to what they've read.

STEPS

1. Use the Story Hand to briefly review with students the three elements they have learned thus far about how stories are made. Then, in a different-colored marker from those used previously, add the word *problem* to a fourth finger. If you're using the Story Hand Buttons template (Appendix, p. 118), glue the appropriate "button" to the problem fingertip.

2. Explain to students that almost every story they'll read will have a problem that needs to be solved. Discuss how we all face problems in our lives—frequent little problems and occasional big problems. Invite students to brainstorm a list of minor problems that might happen in the classroom. Record the list on the left half of a transparency. Here is a sample brainstormed list:

Little Problems We Have in Our Classroom

- Sometimes we forget to share.
- Sometimes we forget to pick up trash.
- Sometimes we break into line.
- Some days we want to go outside, but it's raining.
- The teacher forgets where she has put things!

3. Using the second transparency, brainstorm with the class and record a list of problems in fairy tales or other familiar stories. You might start with the story you used in the previous lesson on plot. Here is a sample list:

Problems in Stories We Know

- ("Cinderella") The prince is hunting for the lady he danced with at the ball.
- ("The Three Little Pigs") The wolf is tearing down the houses and trying to gobble up the pigs.
- ("Hansel and Gretel") The witch is planning to cook Hansel and Gretel in the oven.

4. Finally, read aloud a simple story. Have students listen carefully for a description of the story's problem. When the problem is clearly presented, stop to write it on the third transparency under a new heading, "Problem in Our Story Today," and then finish reading the story. (Keep all three transparency lists available for the final Story Hand lesson.)

FIVE-PART LESSON: GIVE THE STORY A HAND

PART 5: SOLUTION

Explanation

This lesson presents the last story element in the 3-D Story Hand series. Here students discover that problems in stories almost always have satisfying endings—at least in first grade!

Skill Focus

Using graphic/semantic organizers to organize information; identifying story elements (solution); recalling details in text

Materials & Resources

Text

- A narrative text with clear story elements

Other

- The gardening glove used in Parts 1, 2, 3, and 4
- Permanent markers in a variety of colors; glue
- Story Hand Buttons template, optional but highly suggested for English-language learners (Appendix, p. 118)
- The 3 transparencies from Part 4

STEPS

1. Tell students they're now ready for the last ingredient that goes into making a story. With a marker in a different color from those used previously, write the word *solution* on the fifth finger of the Story Hand. If you're using the Story Hand Buttons template (Appendix, p. 118), glue the appropriate "button" to the solution fingertip.

2. Briefly review the discussion about problems. Then challenge students to tell you what a solution is. Guide them to understand that when we have problems, we like to find good solutions. Good solutions make us happy.

3. Call attention to the first transparency used in the previous lesson. Review the list of problems you brainstormed in that lesson about the everyday problems you might encounter or have encountered in your classroom.

4. Create a new column on the transparency and label it "Solutions." With your students, brainstorm solutions that might solve the listed problems. Your list might look like this:

Little Problems We Have in Our Classroom	Solutions
Sometimes we forget to share.	We change and begin to share.
Sometimes we forget to pick up trash.	We pick up trash.
Sometimes we break into line.	We say we are sorry and get in line.
Some days we want to go outside, but it's raining.	We find a fun inside game or read books.
The teacher forgets where she has put things!	We help her remember where things are.

Bonus Ideas

- For each of several familiar stories that the class has read, write a simple description of the problem and the solution on separate sentence strips. Write the title of each story on another strip. Put your collection of strips in a literacy center and challenge students to match the appropriate problems and solutions with the story titles.
- Once the glove has been completed, you can create an easy center activity by placing the Story Hand on a table with several books the class has previously read. Students should select a book and then don the glove to describe to a partner the elements that define that story.

5. Using the second transparency from the Part 4 lesson, follow the same procedure as in Step 4 above. A possible brainstormed list might look like this:

Problems in Stories We Know	Solutions
("Cinderella") The prince is hunting for the lady he danced with at the ball.	He has every lady, including Cinderella, try on the glass slipper.
("The Three Little Pigs") The wolf is tearing down the houses and trying to gobble up the pigs.	The pigs boil a pot of water while the wolf is coming down the chimney.
("Hansel and Gretel") The witch is planning to cook Hansel and Gretel in the oven.	Gretel pushes the witch into the oven.

6. Finally, reread the story you read in the Part 4 lesson. Ask students to listen carefully for the solution. Using the third transparency from the Part 4 lesson, write the story's solution next to the problem the class had identified. Discuss with the class why they feel this was (or was not) a satisfying solution.

DISCOVERING WHAT'S ALIKE AND WHAT'S DIFFERENT

Explanation

Once your students have a good sense of the story elements, they can use this story knowledge to make comparisons both within one story and between different stories. The ability to make these kinds of comparisons is an important critical-thinking skill. This lesson introduces students to a useful matrix graphic organizer that can help them formulate comparisons.

Skill Focus

Using graphic/semantic organizers to organize information; recalling details in text; comparing and contrasting elements within a single text and between two texts

Materials & Resources

Text

- Two stories familiar to students, each with clear story elements (Used in this lesson: "Cinderella" and "Snow White and the Seven Dwarfs")

Other

- Comparing Story Elements chart (Appendix, p. 119), reproduced as a transparency (or you might re-create it, without the illustrations, on a chart or the chalkboard)

Note: *Although this lesson focuses on making comparisons between two different stories, you might choose to introduce the graphic organizer by focusing on the elements from only one book.*

STEPS

1. On a transparency, the board, or poster paper, display a copy of the Comparing Story Elements chart. As students examine it, explain that today the class will fill in the chart with the major elements of two different fairy tales. By doing so, they'll have an opportunity to think in a new way about the way those elements work in each of the stories.

2. Guide students as necessary to help you work your way through each category on the chart, filling in all the major elements of the two stories being compared. Note that the final category of the chart goes beyond the five elements and provides a good opportunity for you to touch on genre identification with students. (See sample completed chart on page 66.)

3. Once the chart has been completed, call students' attention to each horizontal row and challenge students to identify similarities between the two stories. With a colored marker, highlight elements that are close or the same (in the sample chart, these similarities are underlined).

4. Keep blank copies of this chart handy so that individuals or groups of students can use it frequently to compare two stories they have read.

COMPARING STORY ELEMENTS CHART

	Story: "Cinderella"	Story: "Snow White and the Seven Dwarfs"
Characters 	Lonely girl, prince, mean stepmother, fairy godmother	Lonely girl, dwarfs, prince, mean stepmother
Setting 	Stepmother's home, the king's palace, long ago	Stepmother/queen's palace, dwarfs' home in the forest and outside of the forest, long ago
Plot 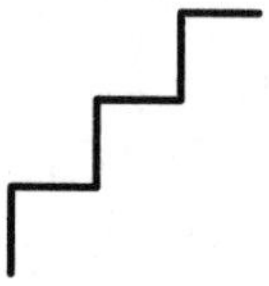	Bullied by her cruel stepmother and stepsisters, Cinderella gets a chance at happiness when her fairy godmother helps her go to the royal ball. The prince is enchanted with Cinderella—but she must rush out of the palace at midnight, leaving her slipper behind; he finds her and they live happily ever after.	Hated by her jealous stepmother the queen, Snow White is banished from the kingdom. She finds happiness with the seven dwarfs, but the evil queen poisons her. Her prince finds her and breaks the spell with a kiss, and they live happily ever after.
Problem 	The prince is hunting for the girl who left her slipper to make her his wife.	Snow White eats the poison apple and falls asleep.
Solution 	The shoe fits Cinderella, and she marries the prince.	The prince finds Snow White, kisses her to wake her from her long sleep, and marries her.
Kind of Story 	Fairy tale	Fairy tale

USING CONCEPT MAPS THAT DESCRIBE AND DEFINE

Explanation

This lesson offers students a modified version of a topic map or web. Rather than the standard circle with satellite bubbles, students' hands are used to create outlines that represent topic (palm) and details (fingers). Because it's so personal, you can bet young students will enjoy this graphic organizer!

Skill Focus

Using graphic/semantic organizers to organize and categorize information; categorizing and classifying words and ideas to build vocabulary

Materials & Resources

Text

- A nonfiction or fiction selection that provides factual knowledge about at least two specific topics (Used in this lesson: *May I Go Out?* by Erin Rosenberg)

Other

- Chart paper (or a transparency or chalkboard)
- For each student: 1 sheet of paper

Bonus Ideas

This activity can be used in many different ways, with both fiction and nonfiction. Students can create hand outlines to show relationships among characters and their traits; settings and relevant details; rocks and their characteristics; planets and what defines them; plants and what they need to grow—the possibilities are endless!

STEPS

1. Read aloud the selection. After discussing it briefly, focus on a topic about which you feel students have gained knowledge from the reading. For example, the sample story takes place in the winter, during a snowstorm. The child discusses with his teacher appropriate clothing for going outdoors in cold and wet weather.

2. Create your model graphic organizer by tracing your hand on the chart paper. On the palm, write a major topic from the text. For example, for the sample story the organizer would look like this:

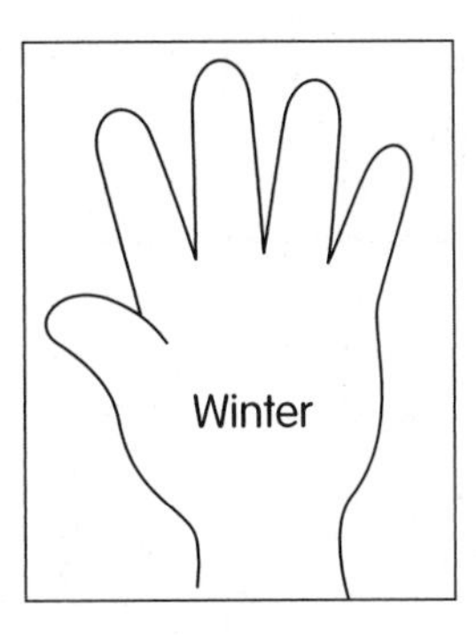

3. Have students brainstorm words that describe or relate to the topic. On each of the fingers of the hand outline, write the brainstormed words. For example, the organizer for the sample story might look like this:

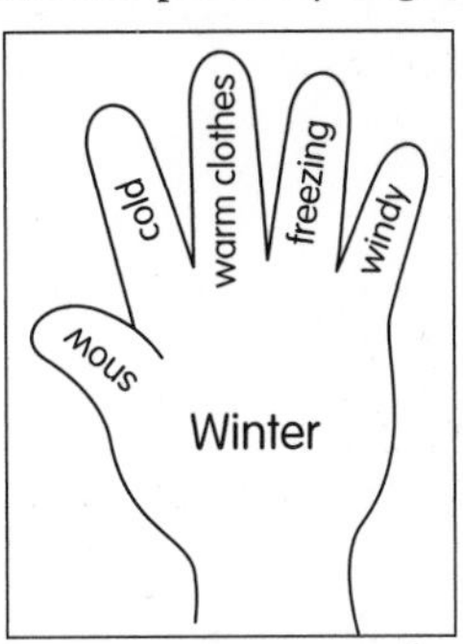

4. Point to the words and discuss them one by one to emphasize the connection between them and the topic written on the palm.

5. Next, give each student a sheet of paper. Have students draw their handprints. Choose another topic from the selection and have students write this word or phrase on the palm. Brainstorm as you did in Step 3, listing words related to the new topic, and have students add these to the fingers. For example, with the sample book, a second likely topic is "Winter Clothes." Brainstormed words might include *scarf*, *coat*, *sweater*, *boots*, and *hats*.

MINI-LESSON

USING CYCLICAL MAPS TO SHOW ORGANIZATION

Explanation

The graphic organizer presented in this lesson depicts circular, or cyclic, structure. This kind of structure is frequently employed in nonfiction text, but it can also apply to fiction. This lesson goes beyond simply having students fill in an organizer—it also involves them kinesthetically in its construction.

Skill Focus

Using graphic/semantic organizers to organize and categorize information; retelling stories; identifying text that uses sequence or other logical order

Materials & Resources

Text

- A nonfiction or fiction selection that is structured according to cyclic order, such as food chains, life cycles, and water cycles (Used in this lesson: the first chapter, "Butterflies and Moths," in *Animal Look-Alikes* by Rachel Griffiths and Margaret Clyne)

Other

- 4 ovals and 4 arrows cut from pastel-colored construction paper (Appendix, p. 120, provides a template)
- Marker; tape

Bonus Ideas

A fun variation on this lesson is to invite students to act out the graphic organizer. Students stand in a circle holding designated ovals and arrows and recite aloud what's written on their part of the organizer.

STEPS

1. Tell students that sometimes a text describes ideas that connect to one another in a circular way. Explain that we call this a *cycle* because one thing leads to another until the cycle returns to the beginning. Today you'll create a graphic map that will show this circle of events.
2. Read to or with your students a selection that depicts a cycle. The sample used in this lesson describes how the egg of the butterfly/moth becomes a caterpillar, which then forms a pupa inside a cocoon. The pupa hatches into the butterfly/moth and the whole process starts again.
3. Display the cut-out paper ovals. With students' input, draw an insect egg on one of the ovals. Attach tape to the back. Invite a student to tape it onto the board, bulletin board, or classroom wall.
4. Now display a cut-out paper arrow. Tell students that the arrow will be used to indicate that the egg is changing into something new. Write on the arrow, "Next it becomes..." Attach tape to the back. Ask a volunteer to add the arrow appropriately (clockwise) to the graphic you're constructing.
5. Draw the next stage, the caterpillar, on another of the ovals and follow the procedure described in Steps 3 and 4. Do the same for the final two stages—the pupa surrounded by its cocoon and the mature butterfly/moth. The final arrow should connect the adult back to the egg again. (See diagram below.)

6. Invite a student to come forward and use your pointer to indicate one set of ovals and arrows. The student should explain what's happening and should focus on how the arrow indicates that a change is occurring.

USING SEQUENTIAL MAPS TO SHOW ORGANIZATION

Explanation

The graphic organizer in this lesson depicts sequential order. It occurs frequently in both fiction and nonfiction and is key structure for young readers to grasp. This lesson gets students actively involved in understanding the organizer by including them kinesthetically in its construction.

Skill Focus

Using graphic/semantic organizers to organize information; retelling stories; identifying text that uses logical order

Materials & Resources

Text

- A nonfiction or fiction selection that is structured according to sequential order (Used in this lesson: *What's for Lunch? Corn* by Pam Robson)

Other

- For each event in the sequence: 1 rectangular shape and 1 arrow shape cut from pastel-colored construction paper (Appendix, p. 121, provides a template)
- Marker; tape

Bonus Ideas

- Keep a supply of cut-out rectangles and arrows in your learning or literacy center, along with both nonfiction and fiction books that highlight sequence. Encourage students to work together in the center to construct a chain of events and to read it aloud with a pointer.

STEPS

1. Explain to students that sometimes a text describes ideas that connect to one another in sequence. *Sequence* means that facts or events follow one another in order: something comes first, next, and last. Today you'll create a graphic map that will show a sequence.

2. Read to or with students a text that is arranged in a sequential fashion. For example, in the sample book, the author takes the reader on a journey from the field where corn is picked to the factory where it is processed and finally to the plate where it is eaten for lunch.

3. Reread the book, stopping at each important event to write that event on a cut-out rectangle. Be as brief as possible in capturing the event and involve the students in the wording as much as possible.

4. Once you have finished the book and recorded all appropriate events, place the rectangles on the floor.

5. Now display the cut-out arrows. On the first, print "FIRST." On ten others, print "NEXT," and on one, print "LAST." Place these on the floor, too.

6. To get the chain started, have a volunteer come forward, select the arrow that says "FIRST," and tape it to the board or wall.

7. Begin to reread or retell the story for the third time and stop when you come to the first event. Have a volunteer come forward, find the rectangle that describes the event you've just read, and tape it near the "FIRST" arrow. Invite another volunteer to follow that student with an arrow that says "NEXT." Proceed this way through subsequent events. Just before the last event, have a volunteer attach the "LAST" arrow and then a final volunteer attach the last event.

8. Reread the chain as you (or a student) use a pointer to follow the sequence. Your students will love the long chain that they've created! A sample completed chain is below.

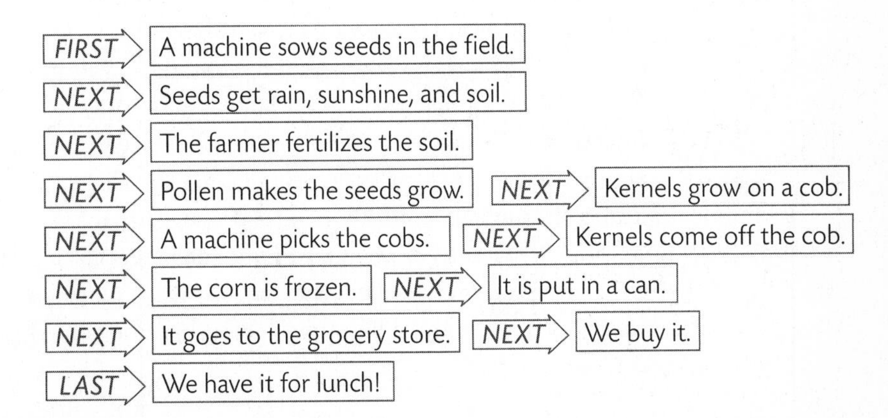

Section Five

Creating and Using Images

Have you ever loved a book and then ventured to the theater expecting to enjoy it even more because of the added dimensions of sight and sound—only to be sorely disappointed that the movie doesn't meet your expectations? This phenomenon may be explained by the fact that good readers visualize what they're reading as they read. As good readers, we've already seen the play or movie in our mind's eye. We've held our own casting of characters, sometimes using people we know or stars we admire. We've already used our own props to establish the setting; we've called on numerous personal experiences and preferences to enrich our understanding of the plot. Then, we see what a Hollywood producer has envisioned for us—and so often it just doesn't match. And, not surprisingly, we like our version better! Most likely, without even consciously realizing it, we've been making use of a sophisticated, essential reading skill—the ability to form images based in part on connections we've made between our own experiences and the text we're reading.

This ability not only makes reading more enjoyable, it enables readers to grow as learners. The research of Gambrell and Koskinen (2002) suggests that there are two great advantages to creating and using mental images when reading: 1) images provide a framework, or "pegs," for organizing and remembering information from texts; and 2) mental images help integrate information across texts. To further understand the importance of visualizing while reading, let's take a look inside a first-grade classroom.

As a first-grade teacher reads *Our Living Forests* by Allan Fowler, children around the room are processing what is heard in many different ways. Two of them—Tricia and Henry—have very little personal knowledge of forests. They live in a suburban town with plantings limited to parks and gardens, and neither student has traveled widely. Tricia, however, has an advantage: she knows how to use the descriptive words in the text to conjure up a reasonable picture of what those places she's hearing about probably look like. Henry listens to *Our Living Forests* intently. He hears the words and he knows individually what they all mean, but he doesn't see pictures as the words are read. He isn't even aware that good readers form pictures in their minds as they read. As a result, Tricia winds up learning new things from this book and extending her knowledge, while Henry gets stuck early on and loses out on an important learning experience.

One of the greatest challenges teachers face in enabling students to create mental images is addressing gaps in prior experiences. But the problem is greatly compounded when children also lack skills and experience in using language to make connections and generate mind pictures. Certainly, both Tricia and Henry can benefit from gaining background knowledge about forests—perhaps through downloaded Internet photos, classroom textbook illustrations, or class discussion involving students who know firsthand about forests. But for Tricia, who already has a profound learning tool available, these instructional experiences will play a different, less fundamental role than for Henry. Like many good readers, from the moment she hears a book's title, she begins to create mental images. And throughout her reading (or listening), Tricia is able to use her knowledge of language to make connections—for example, through analogies or similes—and conjure up images of something she has never seen in real life.

For students like Henry, however, for whom language, imaging skills, and background experiences are all limited, the teacher's job is more difficult. She must provide not only pictures to help him form a knowledge base, but also experience with the language that's related to those pictures before Henry can really make use of them. This can be a time-consuming and challenging task for a teacher, but the impact on the student can be great and the effort can definitely pay off.

The lessons in this section are aimed at helping teachers help students like Henry develop key imaging skills (and at the same time, reinforce these skills for students like Tricia). Imagery training has long proven successful as a way to improve students' memory and inferential reasoning about written text (Levin and Divine-Hawkins, 1974; Borduin et al., 1994). You'll find lessons here on many different aspects of visualizing—from telling stories through illustrations to interpreting nonfiction graphics to highlighting figurative language. So, as we begin this section, let your "good reader" camera roll. You should gain some unique ideas for teaching your students to *see* what they read so that they can better comprehend it.

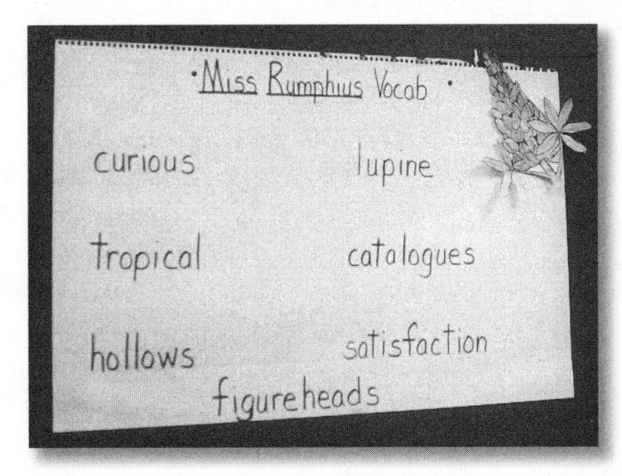

There are many avenues for exploring these new vocabulary words from a favorite narrative text—including having students illustrate the words to get to know them better.

GOING TO THE MOVIES IN YOUR MIND

Explanation

Creating mind pictures as we read is an essential part of good reading. However, for some students, this ability to visualize doesn't come automatically: they don't see the "picture show" in their minds that good readers need to be able to see. This lesson models how to do just that and encourages all your young readers to conjure up images as they read.

Skill Focus

Monitoring comprehension; creating mental and visual images from what is read

Materials & Resources

Text

- An illustrated, narrative text with clear story elements that are easy to visualize (Used in this lesson: *Moonbear's Pet* by Frank Asch)

Bonus Ideas

Invite students to practice visualizing text with their "magic reading sticks" (see page 12). Pair students for reading. Ask them to use their sticks not only in the usual manner–to track print–but also to indicate places where they've formed images. Each time they visualize an image based on something they've read, they should stop the stick and describe the image. This will encourage them to pause and visualize while keeping their places.

STEPS

1. Discuss with students how good readers actually "watch" the story that they're reading. Explain that when you read a good book or story, it can be like going to the movies—only the movie takes place in your mind. Today you're going to model just how that's done.

2. Gather students at the front of the class and hold up the book you've selected. Tell the class you'd like them to sit back and listen to the story. Explain that although the book has some great pictures that the illustrator has drawn, on this reading you're not going to peek at the pictures, nor are you going to show them to the class. Instead, you'll stop and think aloud about the pictures you see in your mind as you read.

3. For example, the sample book starts with Bear finding a new pet in a pond. He tells his friend Little Bird that the new pet is a cute little fish. You might stop here and think aloud something like, "The author has mentioned a character named Bear, one named Little Bird, and a fish. Bear found the fish in a pond. I know that a pond is a pool of water that's small—not large like a lake or a river. So, in my mind I'm seeing a bear standing at the edge of a little pond. I picture him holding a little fish. Oh, and I see a little bird standing at the edge of the pond, too. Now, let me read a little more."

4. Continue to read, stopping frequently to describe aloud pictures that come to your mind.

5. After this reading, go back through the book to show the class the actual illustrations. Point out differences between particular images you had described and the illustrations. Assure students this is just fine—a reader's mind pictures don't always match the illustrator's pictures. Explain that artists read the story, just the way we do, and they see pictures in their own minds before drawing them. Sometimes we might like the illustrator's pictures better, but sometimes we might like the pictures in our minds best of all.

6. After this initial lesson, check in with students occasionally before a read-aloud to ask if they're ready to go to the movies in their minds. You might even suggest that they close their eyes as they listen to you read so that they can see the movie more clearly. Have a good time at the movies!

THE ARTIST'S STORYBOARD

Explanation

In this lesson, you continue to model for students how good readers see in their mind's eye what they read. The lesson also taps the natural artistic talents of your students as it encourages them to visualize and illustrate stories they have read.

Skill Focus

Monitoring comprehension; creating mental and visual images from what is read; retelling stories; using graphic representations (pictures) as a means of organizing information and events logically

Materials & Resources

Text

- A narrative text with clear story elements that are easy to visualize (Used in this lesson: *Miss Smith's Incredible Storybook* by Michael Garland)

Other

- Artist's Storyboard (Appendix, p. 122)
- Chart paper

Bonus Ideas

You can also use the storyboard concept with informational text. Of course, you won't include story elements, but instead you'll draw the facts and other ideas you've learned from that text selection.

STEPS

1. Review the importance of readers' visualizing scenes and characters as they read a story. Remind the class that an illustrator doesn't typically talk with an author to find out exactly what he or she intended to portray. Book illustrators base their drawings only on the movies they see in their minds as they read the author's words. Tell students you're going to read a story today and draw what you see just as if you were an illustrator.

2. Gather students near a large blank sheet of poster paper. Create a storyboard chart by drawing four lines vertically and then three lines horizontally to divide the chart into thirds. This will give you a symmetrical chart with six cells for the drawings, of which you'll need five for the sample story (see step 3). Note that because many stories may have more events, the Appendix template provides eight cells.

3. Begin reading the story aloud. When you've read enough to get an impression, stop and illustrate it on the chart. Try to depict these elements: main character, setting, an event that shows the problem, an event that shows the solution, and the ending event. (Don't be intimidated if you feel artistically challenged. It won't matter to your students. Your illustrations are guaranteed to entertain them! Also, if you're artistically challenged, you'll validate those students who also worry that their drawings won't be acceptable.) A plot summary of the sample story and a description of the storyboard based on that plot follow:

   Plot Summary: This delightful story is about a teacher who has a talent for bringing books alive for her students. One day when she's away from school, the principal comes to the class to read to the students. He brings the stories alive but can't get the characters to return to the books! Miss Smith reappears and saves the day.

   Artist's Storyboard

Here's the main character . . .	First . . .	Here's an event . . .
Your sketch of Miss Smith, labeled as "Miss Smith"	Your sketch of a book showing a dog and cat coming out	Your sketch of same book with swirled lines to indicate the dog and cat returning to the book
Here's an event . . .	**Here's what happens at the end . . .**	
Your sketch of a man, an open book, and several animals near the man	Your sketch of Miss Smith, alone, with the closed book in her hands and swirled lines around it to show movement	

4. After the chart is complete, reread the story or just flip back through the book and retell the events. Either way, display the illustrations this time.

5. As follow-up to this lesson, make available to students copies of the Artist's Storyboard (see Appendix, p. 122). Encourage them to draw what they see as they read stories on their own or as they hear stories read aloud. With your students' permission, you may occasionally want to display their storyboards for other classes.

CREATING WORD PICTURES

Explanation

Most teachers realize early on that there's little retention of vocabulary words when students simply memorize definitions. In this lesson, students will have an opportunity to process words in a different way—a way that will ensure both greater comprehension and retention.

Skill Focus

Monitoring comprehension; creating mental and visual images from what is read; developing vocabulary through meaningful/concrete experiences

Materials & Resources

Text

- A fiction or nonfiction text that includes several concrete (rather than abstract) vocabulary words

Other

- For each student: 1 sheet of unlined paper

Bonus Ideas

For units of study, you might bind together these sheets of illustrations and words to form "pictionaries" that can be used as resources in the classroom.

STEPS

1. Tell students that in today's lesson you will focus on a helpful way to remember new vocabulary words. Remind the class that they have been learning about the importance of visualizing as they read. This lesson gives them another reason to visualize: by drawing new vocabulary words, they will find that they can remember these words more easily.

2. Distribute to each student a sheet of unlined paper. Have them fold the sheet in half (either widthwise or lengthwise), and then in half again. Instruct them to press the creases well.

3. Now have students unfold the paper. They should have a piece of paper with creases that divide it into four equal segments.

4. Read aloud your preselected text; it should contain at least several new concrete vocabulary words. For example, in a book about how caterpillars change into moths, you would encounter the word *cocoon*. At the word's first occurrence, stop reading and discuss aspects of a cocoon with the class—how it might look, how large it is, what color it is, and so on. You might also ask if anyone has ever seen a cocoon and share a picture of one.

5. Ask students to select a section of their paper and to write the word *cocoon* within that section, using no more than half of the space for the word. Within the remaining part of that section, have them draw a picture that will remind them of what a cocoon is. Depending upon your individual class needs, you might model the procedure ahead of time or simply work along with students to fill in your own section. An example is at right.

cocoon	

6. Continue in this manner with additional words until you finish the selection. Note: If your text selection includes more than four words, you can either turn the paper over and use the four segments on the back or you can have the students fold the paper in half three times, rather than two, to create a grid of eight equal parts.

GETTING TO KNOW YOUR WORDS

Explanation

Here's another lesson that helps students process vocabulary in so many varied ways—including visual and even silly ways—that they come to truly know and own the new words. The form introduced in the lesson can be used frequently to help students amass their own personal store of vocabulary words.

Skill Focus

Monitoring comprehension; creating mental and visual images from what is read; developing vocabulary through meaningful/concrete experiences

Materials & Resources

Text

- A fiction or nonfiction text that includes several new vocabulary words (Used in this lesson: *A Look at Spiders* by Jerald Halpern)

Other

- For each student: 1 Know Your Words form (Appendix, p. 123)
- Transparency of the same form
- An assortment of colored transparency pens

Bonus Ideas

Once students are familiar with this method, you can send several volunteers to the board quickly when the class encounters an important vocabulary word. Assign one student to draw, one to build, one to color, and one to write it.

***Note:** For your modeling, choose a word that's critical to the comprehension of the reading selection. In the sample book for this lesson, the word* tunnel *is key. It occurs in a discussion that describes how spiders spin silk and line underground tunnels.*

STEPS

1. Tell students that today's lesson will help them to really get to know a new vocabulary word. By experiencing the word in all the ways that this lesson affords, they will truly experience and come to "own" that word. Knowing the word will not only help them understand what they're now reading, but it will become a new word in their personal vocabularies forever.

2. Read the text aloud. Write the word *tunnel* at the top of the transparency.

3. In the first box, "Draw It," draw a simple tunnel, which in this context would be a long hole dug down in the earth.

4. In the next box, "Build on It," analyze any familiar word parts or simple opportunities to change the word to make a slightly new word. For *tunnel*, you might point to the letters *un* and say, "I'm looking for word parts here. But, I'm not going to be tricked by this! I know that *un-* is added to the beginnings of lots of words—as in *unhappy*, where *un-* is added to *happy* to completely change the meaning. But here *un-* is in the middle of the word and it doesn't work that way. So, instead of highlighting that, I'm going to do something different in this 'Build' box. I'm going to add an *s* to *tunnel* and turn it into more than one tunnel. I know that works!"

5. In the next box, "Color It," select a color that might commonly be associated with the word. For example, you might tell your students that because the spider's tunnel would be in the ground, you'll use brown. You can simply color the whole box brown or draw the tunnel again and color it. (Note: Variations are possible here. For example, students might draw something related to the word and/or they might use a color that expresses how the word makes them feel.)

6. Now call attention to the "Write It" box. Demonstrate for students how you have fun writing the word in some unusual way—perhaps in a different style, by boxing the letters, or by giving it eyes and personifying it!

7. For the "Use It in a Sentence" box, make up a simple sentence like "Spiders line tunnels with silk," and write it within the box.

8. The dotted, unlabeled box can be used for something uniquely appropriate to the word—for instance, a synonym, antonym, homonym, or rhyme. For *tunnel*, you might write *funnel* and draw a small picture of a funnel.

9. Distribute Know Your Words forms (Appendix, p. 123). Based on independent reading books, have students follow your model to complete the form.

Reading the Pictures

Explanation

Young children are naturally drawn to visuals on book pages that have both text and pictures. They may not place the same value on them, however, unless we stress that pictures must be "read" just as text is. This lesson engages them in a fun activity that teaches them to scrutinize and learn from pictures when there is no text on a page to fall back on.

Skill Focus

Monitoring comprehension; creating mental and visual images from what is read; developing vocabulary through meaningful/ concrete experiences; using graphic representations such as charts, graphs, pictures, and graphic organizers as information sources

Materials & Resources

Text

- An informational text, such as your science, social studies, or other content book, with graphics as well as text (Used in this lesson: *Splish, Splash, Splosh!* by Mick Manning and Brita Granstrom)

Other

- Several sticky notes
- For each student: 1 photocopy of a prepared page from the text used in this lesson

Prior to the Lesson: *First, from your selected book, choose a page on which graphics convey important information that is also described in the text. Don't use the first couple of pages. You'll want your students to build a good understanding first before trying to interpret meaning from pictures. Use sticky notes to cover all the words on your chosen page, leaving only the graphics (photographs, graphs, charts, illustrations). Next, choose another page (if possible, immediately following the original page) on which the graphics convey key information that is also described in the text. Using sticky notes, prepare this page just as you did the first. Make photocopies (one for each student) of this now-wordless page. Be sure to leave the sticky notes in place on the original after you have made the photocopies.*

Steps

1. Explain that we can read pictures in books, just as we can read text. By examining the pictures carefully, we can learn a great deal of information about the topic we are studying. Today you're going to challenge the class to learn as much as they can from just the pictures on a page.

2. Share the cover or title of your selected text and discuss briefly the topic of the text. Be sure that you help students tap into or generate prior knowledge about the topic so that they can better connect to the text.

3. Read the text aloud. Stop at the first page you've covered with sticky notes. Display the page, which will have only graphics visible. Model how you think aloud about the picture(s). For example, with the sample book, you might stop at the double-page picture on pages 18 and 19 and say, "This picture is familiar to me. I think it's a house in a neighborhood just like mine. The illustrator has cut away part of the side of this house to show us what's happening in lots of the rooms. We know that this book is about water. I think the illustrator is showing us the different uses for water in our homes. The water is coming through pipes into the kitchen sink where we wash dishes, into the shower where we bathe, and into the toilet that we flush. The other page is showing the very long pipes that the water has to travel through to get into our homes. Wow! I don't often stop to think about where the water in our homes comes from, do you?"

4. Now, peel away the sticky notes and read the words on that page to confirm what you've read in the pictures.

5. Continue to read until you reach the next page that you've prepared. Distribute the photocopies of this page. Ask students to take a minute to "read" the picture. You might divide them into pairs to discuss what they think is happening on that page. Or they might write out their interpretation of the picture in the blank space on the page.

6. Gather students to share what they've read in the pictures. Then, remove the sticky notes from the actual book page and read aloud the text.

STOP, LOOK, AND TELL

Explanation

You need to do all that you can to get children to actively visualize and create personal mind pictures during reading. This is a fun lesson that will help students focus on and "see" what they're reading in a new and different way!

Skill Focus

Monitoring comprehension; creating mental and visual images from what is read; developing vocabulary through meaningful/concrete experiences; recalling details in texts

Materials & Resources

Text

- A fiction or nonfiction text that includes several descriptive passages

Other

- For each student: tag-paper eyeglass frames (cut from pattern in Appendix, p. 118) and 2 short (or 1 long) pipe cleaner(s)
- Markers, stickers, and/or crayons
- Hole puncher

Bonus Ideas

Suggest that students also use these special glasses to "read the room." Set up a designated time for them to move about the classroom with a partner or a small group. They should use their magic reading sticks to point to various text selections and examples in the classroom while wearing their new glasses to read the text.

Prior to the Lesson: *Using tag paper and the template in the Appendix, page 118, cut out an eyeglass frame for each student. Punch a hole in each side (students will attach pipe cleaners to these holes).*

STEPS

1. Briefly review the importance of creating mind pictures as we read. Tell students that it sometimes helps to have a reminder of important things we need to do. So today, they're going to help make their own personal "picture show" eyeglass frames. Every time they put on these frames, they'll be reminded that they need to compose pictures in their mind of what they're reading.

2. Give each student an eyeglass frame. Make art supplies available and invite students to decorate and personalize their glasses. Use this opportunity to create your own pair of designer glasses as well!

3. Help students attach pipe cleaners to the punched holes. Adjust earpieces for each student.

4. Put on your new glasses. Model for students how you use the glasses to remind yourself to visualize what you're reading. Read aloud a brief selection, then stop and describe what you are picturing in your mind. Say something like, "What a help these glasses are! They're reminding me to stop and to take the time to really see a picture in my mind of what I'm reading."

5. Have students put on their own glasses. Continue to read the text until you come to the next descriptive passage. Tell students that you want them to spend a moment "looking" at the picture in their minds silently. Then have them tell a buddy what they were able to see with the help of their special glasses.

6. Introduce the phrase "Stop, Look, and Tell" to students and point out that this is what they just did with the passage you read. Continue reading to the end of the selection. Call out the phrase at appropriate spots and have students follow the procedure described in Step 5.

7. As students mature as readers, they won't need the glasses as reminders. But continue throughout the year to use the "Stop, Look, and Tell" method for calling attention to what students can and should visualize in their minds' eye.

BECOMING THE STORY

Explanation

In this lesson, visual and kinesthetic approaches support students as they grow into more mature readers. Students are asked to visualize a text, to imagine themselves not only as characters but also as important items and objects, and then to put on an impromptu production of the story.

Skill Focus

Creating mental and visual images from what is read; responding to reading through acting and creative dramatics

Materials & Resources

Text

- A short, simple narrative text that has at least four or five characters and a number of concrete objects and items (Used in this lesson: *How Spiders Got Eight Legs* by Katherine Mead)

Other

- For each actor: 2-gallon sealing bag; about 2 feet of ribbon or string; 1 sheet of colored construction paper; either a picture or printed name of the actor's character/item (see right for directions)

Bonus Ideas

Students can also create impromptu dramas by drawing the characters or finding likenesses in magazines, cutting them out, and gluing them to dowels or art sticks. Then, as the story is reread, they can move the stick figures like puppets to show the action. Keep it simple and it will be even more fun for students!

Prior to the Lesson: *Do one of the following: photocopy from the book and enlarge a picture of each character/item that students will portray; or freehand-draw each item/character on a full sheet of paper; or write the character's/item's name on a full sheet of paper. To each picture or word, glue a sheet of colored construction paper to form a backing. Insert the picture or word in the seal-lock bag. Punch holes in the top left and right corners of the bag. Insert the string or ribbon so that the bag can hang loosely around the neck of each actor.*

You might want to refer to a related lesson (page 114) for further ideas about dramatizing.

STEPS

1. Tell students that another way they can deepen their understanding of a story and better visualize what the story is really about is by acting out the story. In this lesson, they will get a chance to "become the story." Explain that becoming the story involves more than just acting out the characters' parts; it also means that they might choose to be the props—the background items and objects—to help the story come to life.

2. Read aloud, and then reread, a story to or with your students. Discuss the story and help the class develop a solid understanding of what takes place.

3. Gather students around a chart and elicit what they see in the story. List all of the items they mention that are concrete enough to include in a production of the story. For example, a list for the sample book might include:

Spider	Ostrich	Trees	Giraffe
Cheetah	Great Hippo	Boulders	

4. Choose students to portray various roles. (If you have a particularly "dramatic" class and too many volunteers for this one story, consider repeating this activity on another day so that all students have a chance to participate actively.)

5. Place the appropriate name card or picture around the neck of each character and introduce them, one by one. Go through the story, highlighting key events. Talk about how and when different characters appear.

6. Finally, read the story as students act it out. At the end, be sure to praise your students for showing you so clearly what they visualized as they first heard this story.

FIGURES OF SPEECH: HOW WRITERS CREATE IMAGES

Explanation

This lesson invites students to watch for an author's use of special, descriptive language (figures of speech). The lesson focuses on how figurative language can help readers form mind pictures. There's no need to classify or label figures of speech for emergent readers. At this point, what they need is a general sense of the special effects created by language on the printed page.

Skill Focus

Creating mental and visual images from what is read; identifying devices of figurative language such as similes and metaphors

Materials & Resources

Text

- A text that includes figures of speech that suggest clear images (Used in this lesson: *Kitten's First Full Moon* by Kevin Henkes; also recommended: *Quick As a Cricket* by Audrey Wood)

Other

- List of partially completed figures of speech—either as a transparency or simply as a reference for writing on the board

Bonus Ideas

Play a game of "Good Picture/Bad Picture" with students to encourage them to be more discerning as they come up with their own comparisons. In addition to effective comparisons, give them some that don't work—like "as colorful as dirt." Challenge them to decide whether each comparison creates a good or bad picture and to tell why.

STEPS

1. Explain to students that authors often help readers see pictures in their minds by using words in a special way. Instead of expecting the readers to figure out all on their own how something looks, they give the reader clues in a clever way! Ask students to be detectives and look for the clues in the book you're going to read to them.

2. Before reading your selected text, pose some leading questions. For example, for the sample book, you might ask, "What do you think the author will say the moon looks like? Use your imaginations to guess what a kitten might think the moon is as he looks at it. What do you think?" Encourage students to volunteer ideas.

3. Start reading the story aloud to students. Ask them to raise their hands as soon as they know what the author says the moon looks like. As students raise their hands, stop reading and have them turn to a partner quickly to say what the moon looked liked to the kitten (a bowl of milk, which the kitten wants to get). If appropriate, follow up at this point with another question. For the sample book, you might ask why the title used the words *full moon* rather than just *moon* (the moon, when full, would look more like a bowl of milk than it would during other phases).

4. Finish reading the book aloud for students' enjoyment. Then tell the class you want them to use their imaginations just as authors do. Present your list of partially completed figures of speech. Encourage volunteers to complete these statements and record their suggestions. Following is one sample list:

   Her coat was as colorful as ___________________.

   When he woke up, his hair looked like ___________________.

   The tulip was shaped like a ______________________.

   He ran as quickly as ________________________.

   She was as quiet as ________________________.

5. Remind students to be on the lookout in all their reading for special, descriptive words and comparisons that help them visualize images.

Section Six

Accessing Prior Knowledge

We now know that reading is an active process of meaning construction in which readers connect old knowledge with new information they encounter in the text (Harris and Hodges, 1995). If we envision this process as a formula, it would be: old knowledge plus new knowledge equals comprehension. Thinking about it this way helps to highlight two important factors involved in teaching young readers. First, students often assume they have a one-way relationship with the printed page: it's there to tell them everything. An important part of the teacher's job is to help students realize they bring a great deal to the page. Rather than one-way, the relationship is always interactive. Second, because every reader brings a different, indeed unique, constellation of experiences and knowledge to the page, every reader is reading and comprehending uniquely.

The lessons in this section are primarily intended to help you develop the first factor—students' ability to call upon and make use of the background knowledge that they already have. Before saying a bit more about that, it's important to point out that frequently a teacher must go beyond helping students retrieve knowledge and must, in addition, actually help them build that knowledge. Many children, especially low achievers, have had limited experiences in their young lives. They have significant gaps in their exposure to text and world knowledge.

Good teachers are aware of this with every lesson they teach, realizing that a key part of their work is to help such students lay that all-important foundation. If the class is studying Egypt and some students have never left the boundaries of their community, a teacher needs to pull down the map, go to the Internet to do research, show them pictures, and engage them in discussions to provide experiences that will help to make them successful. Only when the reader can associate a text with memories and experiences does it become anchored in the reader's mind (Keene and Zimmermann, 1997). Staying mindful of this daily certainly takes effort on the teacher's part. But when comprehension is the reward, the payoff for both student and teacher is immense and worth all the effort.

You'll find that the lessons in this section use different ways to tap (and sometimes to build upon) students' prior knowledge. Sometimes you'll ask students to retrieve what they know and add to it through conversations with their classmates. Sometimes they'll be using anticipation guides to declare before reading what they feel they know about a topic. In other lessons, you'll ask them to make different kinds of connections—text-to-self, text-to-text, and text-to-the-world—to get ready for reading with comprehension. And in a few lessons, students will have the chance to use graphics—charts and webs—to aid them in retrieving what they know.

Let's take a look now at different ways you can prepare students to approach the printed page. Your goal is clear: to give them a better sense of how what they already know can help them come away from the page knowing even more.

Memory squares are a wonderful way for students to demonstrate connections between their personal lives and a text. This is one square from the "quilt" shown on page 80.

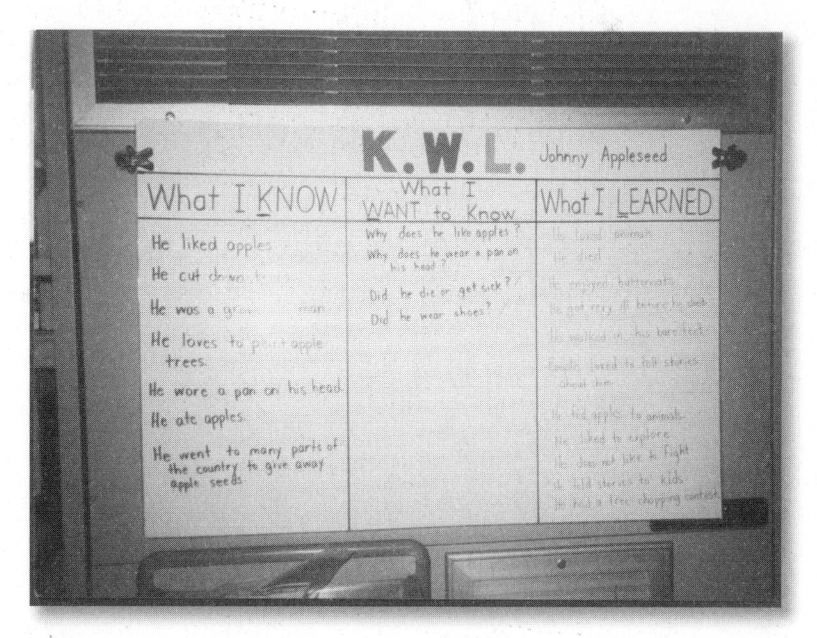

A class has used a KWL chart to help them focus on prior knowledge and new learning about Johnny Appleseed.

BUZZING WITH OUR BUDDIES

Explanation

In first grade, children's use of oral language is still their fastest means of communication—probably no great revelation to their teachers! This lesson capitalizes on those oral language skills and connects students to a text they're about to read or listen to. And it provides you with a yearlong technique to help students activate prior knowledge.

Skill Focus

Making connections among texts read aloud or independently and prior knowledge, other texts, and the world

Materials & Resources

Text

- A grade-appropriate narrative or informational text

Other

- 1 sheet of poster board
- Bee Outline (Appendix, p. 124)
- Yellow cardstock
- Black wide-tip marker
- Glue

Bonus Ideas

Here are three hints for further use of Buzz Buddies: a) it's helpful to change the groups every month or quarter so students get different perspectives; b) use Buzz Buddies just before students write about self-selected topics so that they are exposed to many potential ideas for writing; c) use Buzz Buddies in all your content areas to activate students' prior knowledge about topics.

Prior to the Lesson: *Using the Bee Outline (Appendix, p. 124), cut out bee shapes (one bee for every three students) from the yellow cardstock.*

STEPS

1. With students gathered around you, mount the poster board on an easel or tape it to the chalkboard. Using the black marker, title the chart "Buzz Buddies." Tell students that for the rest of the school year, each of them will have several Buzz Buddies. Explain that *buzz* is another word for *talk*, because when many people are talking, it can sound like bees buzzing. So these are going to be special buddies with whom you'll expect students to chat during reading lessons.

2. Glue the bee shapes onto the poster board. Write students' names in groups of about three on each of the bees. (Groups of three work best, but if necessary, you can place up to four students in a group. Also, it's best if you decide on the grouping yourself. When students do the choosing, often it's the children who most need the buddies who get left out.)

3. Explain to students that from now on, reading lessons may often involve Buzz Buddy chats. You'll ask them questions or give them topics to discuss, and then you'll instruct them to "Sit with your Buzz Buddies." At that point, they should hurry to their group to chat for the time you've allotted—sometimes only a minute or two. (To streamline the time, choose a consistent meeting place for each group.)

4. Tell the class that today you're going to model what a buzz group does. Call on two of your more perceptive, engaged students to help you. Say something like, "Imagine we're about to read a new informational book about butterflies, and I ask you to find your Buzz Buddies to share quickly some things that you already know about butterflies. I'm going to sit with Shannon and Lisa to tell them something I know about butterflies and to hear what they know."

5. Sit in a small circle with the two students you've chosen and set your timer for about two minutes. Share facts you might know about butterflies. Be sure the two students get a chance to speak so that the modeling really appears to be group chatting. When time is up, have the two students return to their desks. Tell the class, "So this is exactly what you'll do. When I give the word, just before a reading assignment, you'll meet with the other students whose names are written on the same bee as your name. You'll need to be sure that everyone gets to say something on the topic when we buzz."

6. Conclude by giving a reading assignment. Hold your first Buzz Buddies session before the reading so that students can practice right away.

ANTICIPATION

Explanation

"Long, long ago" (about three decades ago, to be precise) anticipation guides were the rage. Well, as they say, what goes around comes around! The anticipation guide is back and working as well as ever. This lesson offers a variation for first graders and gives your young readers a chance to find out how much they know about a topic before reading.

Skill Focus

Making connections among texts read aloud or independently and prior knowledge, other texts, and the world; making and confirming predictions about text

Materials & Resources

Text

- A grade-appropriate informational text (Used in this lesson: *Rockets and Spaceships* by Karen Wallace)

Other

- For each student: 1 small piece of paper

Bonus Ideas

Based on what they're reading, students can generate their own true and false statements and quiz classmates with their statements. To help them prepare, show them how to change a fact into a false statement. They'll be eager to fool their friends!

STEPS

1. Discuss with students that all readers bring a great deal of knowledge to each reading selection. This knowledge really helps readers understand what the selection means. Today they'll get to show what they already know or at least make a guess about what they think they know. They may be surprised to find that they know more than they think they do!

2. Tell students that you're going to read aloud a good book about space travel. First you want students to decide if certain statements about space travel are true or false. Then they'll have a chance to listen to the book and decide if those same statements actually are true or false.

3. On a transparency or the board, draw a three-column chart. Title the left column "Before Reading"; the middle "Statement: True or False?"; and the right column "After Reading." Add the words *Yes* and *No* underneath the titles of the middle and right columns. (See example in Step 4.) Tell students that for each statement you read, they should put up their thumbs if they think it's true and they should turn down their thumbs if they think the statement or some part of it is not true. Stress that you want them to guess even if they aren't sure. They should all respond to each sentence.

4. Now read aloud (and repeat, if you wish) each of your prepared statements. Write each on the chart as you read it. Give students a little "think time" and then ask, "Thumbs up or thumbs down?" Under the "Before Reading" column, record the number of "yes" and "no" votes. See sample chart. (Note that in this sample, numbers 2 and 3 are false statements.)

Rockets and Spaceships **by Karen Wallace**

Before Reading	Statement: True or False?		After Reading	
	Yes	No	Yes	No
1. Rockets take spaceships to space and then they fall away.				
2. The plane part of a space shuttle can be used only once.				
3. Most space scientists are called rocket riders.				
4. Probes are machines that do not carry people.				
5. The plane part of a space shuttle lands back on Earth like an airplane.				

5. Distribute a small piece of paper to each student and direct students to write the numbers 1–5. Tell them you're now going to read aloud the book. They need to listen carefully for the targeted statements and to decide whether those statements are actually true or false. Next to each number, they should write *Yes* if it's true and *No* if they think it's false. After the reading, ask for a show of hands for the verdict on each statement.

6. Go back over the statements and review actual text information as needed to clarify answers and to explain any discrepancies or confusion.

CONNECTING WITH WHAT YOU KNOW

Explanation

This lesson introduces students to a tried-and-true technique, the topic map/web. This kind of map is especially valuable in helping students retrieve what they already know as they approach a text and prepare for reading. The connection highlighted in this lesson is text-to-self, a relatively easy connection for first graders to make.

Skill Focus

Making connections among texts read aloud or independently and prior knowledge, other texts, and the world; making and confirming predictions about text; using graphic/semantic organizers to organize and categorize information

Materials & Resources

Text

- A grade-appropriate narrative or informational text (Used in this lesson: *Making the World* by Douglas Wood)

STEPS

1. Tell students that good readers look carefully at titles, headings, covers, and pictures to make connections to and predictions about what they'll be reading. This helps them think about the topic or the story they're about to read and get ready to read with better understanding.

2. Display the book you've selected and call students' attention to the title and the cover illustration. For example, with the sample book, you might say, "I see a boy sitting on the sand with a bucket and shovel. In the background I see water and waves. I think this is taking place at the ocean. My family goes to the ocean every summer. Sometimes we sit in the sand with small buckets and shovels to make sand castles. We have so much fun! I think that my experience at the beach might help me to understand this story better because it's something I know about."

3. On a transparency or the board, draw a topic map, placing the title of the text in the middle of the map. Fill in one of the satellite ovals with the experience you've described. Say something like, "I'm going to draw a line between my experience and the story to show that I think there will be a connection."

4. Ask students if any have had experiences related to the beach scene depicted. As students share experiences that relate to the topic, add satellite ovals to the map. If students go off track, you might occasionally inquire, "Do you think that connects to what we'll read about today?" to help keep them focused. One possible topic map for the sample book is below:

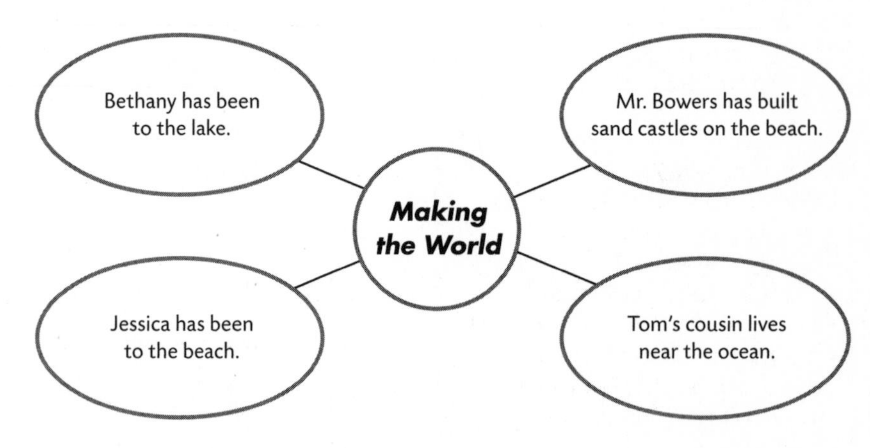

5. Read your selected book aloud. Then return to the topic map you've created and review it with the class to help them see how their experiences prepared them to better understand the story.

Connecting With Something You've Read

Explanation

This lesson highlights another connection that we want students to make readily as they begin to read–text-to-text. With all the reading and exposure to books that students experience in a first-grade classroom, text-to-text connections should be made frequently.

Skill Focus

Making connections among texts read aloud or independently and prior knowledge, other texts, and the world; making and confirming predictions about text

Materials & Resources

Text

- A grade-appropriate narrative or informational text (Used in this lesson: *Rockets and Spaceships* by Karen Wallace)

Other

- Sticky notes

Bonus Ideas

On the board or a poster, sketch two outlines of opened books, their front and back covers spread out from the spine. Link the two with a chalk-drawn line or yarn. Invite students to use this graphic to make connections between two books they've read. They should write the titles of the books in the space within each outline, with a brief note explaining the connection.

Steps

1. Review with students what they learned in the previous lesson—that good readers look carefully at titles, headings, covers, and pictures to make predictions about the topic or story they're going to read. Remind them that the previous lesson focused on the way readers use personal experiences to make connections and predictions. Explain that that's only one kind of possible connection. Sometimes readers may not personally have had an experience that helps them understand the text. Then they can think about other books or texts they've read to help them.

2. Display your selected text and show students how you examine the cover and the title. For example, with the sample text you might say, "From the title and the picture on the cover, I'm sure this book is going to be about rockets and other space vehicles that leave Earth to travel in space. Although I think it would be fun to go into space, that's certainly not an experience I've had!" Write the book's title on the board and add something like, "I know we've read about planets and rockets in our science book. So I might use what I've learned from that book about space to help me better understand *this* book."

3. On a sticky note, write the title or a phrase that refers to the other book. Place it near the title on the board. For this sample lesson, the teacher would write "Our science book" on the sticky note. Draw a line between the note and the title and say something like, "What I learned from our science book will help to connect me to this new book. So, I'm drawing a line to connect them."

4. You might wish to add another resource. Explain, "I also remember a book we read by Gail Gibbons called *The Moon Book*. I'll bet that will help me understand *Rockets and Spaceships* better, too!" Jot down "*The Moon Book*" on another sticky note. Place the sticky note near the title of today's selection and draw a line to connect the two.

5. Ask students if they've read anything that will help them connect to today's book. List their books on additional sticky notes and place them near the title. If students don't remember specific text titles, you might jot down a brief description instead.

6. Sum up with students that so far they've learned two ways that they can activate what they already know (their prior knowledge) before reading: a) recalling experiences they've had, and b) remembering other things they've read on the same topic.

CONNECTING WITH THE WORLD AROUND US

Explanation

This lesson looks at the third of the three basic ways that we connect with text: through events that go on around us that we've seen or heard about. Because this third category is the broadest and most abstract, it is also often the most difficult for first graders to grasp. Nonetheless, they can handle this critical concept if it is modeled clearly and reinforced frequently for them.

Skill Focus

Making connections among texts read aloud or independently and prior knowledge, other texts, and the world; making and confirming predictions about text

Materials & Resources

Text

- A grade-appropriate narrative or informational text (Used in this lesson: *Fly Away Home* by Eve Bunting)

STEPS

1. Review with students the types of connections you've studied so far: connections that are personal and connections based on what they've read. Refresh their understanding by going over examples of each of these connections. Be sure to stress that all of a reader's connections are individual. For example, for a story that takes place at the beach, some students might be able to call to mind their own beach experiences, while other students, who have never been to a beach, might have read a book about the beach and might be able to make a connection that way. Still other students might have been to the beach themselves as well as read about it in a book. So they would have two sources for making connections.

2. Explain that today you'll show students how to make a third kind of connection. These kinds of connections are called "text-to-world." They aren't connected to something we've experienced ourselves or to a book we've read before. Instead, they come from our knowledge of the world—the way the world works or perhaps something we know that's happened in the world.

3. Display your selected text and model for students how you examine the cover and the title. For example, with the sample text you might say, "From the title and the picture on the cover, I can tell that this story is taking place in an airport. I've been in lots of airports so I wonder if my experiences will be like these characters'? I've made a text-to-self connection so far."

4. Continue to read the story. When it becomes clear that the boy and his father are homeless, say something like, "I can see this is the story of a young boy and his father who are living in an airport. This isn't making me think of anything in my own experience, but this story has made me think of what happened after a terrible hurricane hit New Orleans, Louisiana, in 2005. Many thousands of people were left without homes there. I saw on television how generous people all around the country acted. They invited the people whose houses were destroyed to come and stay in their homes. I'll bet many of those people felt just like this young boy and his father who had no place to call their own. I've made a text-to-world connection to help me understand what's happening in the story and how the characters must feel."

5. Especially because these kinds of connections are more abstract for young readers to grasp, redefine the term a "text-to-world connection" and invite class discussion about the concept. Be sure to keep in mind that identifying what types of connection being made isn't what's most important with first graders. What is key is that they make all three kinds of connections to help them activate prior knowledge and better comprehend text.

KWLW CHARTS

Explanation

By now students should understand that as readers they bring a great deal to the page. This activity not only encourages students to retrieve what they already knew prior to reading but also promotes a great deal of thoughtful interaction with the text during and after reading.

Skill Focus

Making connections among texts read aloud or independently and prior knowledge, other texts, and the world; making and confirming predictions about text; using graphic/semantic organizers to organize and categorize information

Materials & Resources

Text

- A grade-appropriate nonfiction/informational text about a topic somewhat familiar to students (Used in this lesson: *Splish, Splash, Splosh!* by Mick Manning and Brita Granstrom)

Other

- Sticky notes

Bonus Ideas

Transfer questions that remain in the "What We Still Wonder" column to a classroom chart that you've titled "We Wonder." These questions make good starters for classroom discussions and great topics for inspiring students' own writing!

STEPS

1. Remind students that readers bring prior knowledge to their reading and they also learn from it. Tell the class that good readers also wind up with new questions after they've finished their reading. Today, students will have a chance to sort out all these different ways they relate to text.

2. Display the cover of the book you've selected. Give each student a sticky note and tell them to use the note to either write or draw something they already know about this topic. Model this with the sample book. Say, "From the title and cover, I can see that this book is about water. I know that there is a water tower near my house where the city stores water that comes to our homes. I'm going to sketch a picture of a tower."

3. On a transparency or the board, draw this chart:

What We Already Know	What We Want to Learn	What We Learned	What We Still Wonder

4. Place your sticky note on the board under the "What We Already Know" column. Invite a few students to share their own sticky notes aloud and to place their notes on the chart. Ask the remaining students to share with a buddy and then to place their sticky notes on the board.

5. Next, think aloud about what you want to learn from this book. Explain that you realize your questions may or may not be answered, but the important point is that the topic already has gotten you to think about these questions. You might say, "I've never totally understood how the water gets to my house. I would like to know that. I'm going to sketch a house with a question mark beside it." Place your new sticky note in the column under "What We Want to Learn."

6. Invite students to think of questions they might have about the topic and to again come up to place their sticky notes in the correct column. Share some of the questions aloud (this will help set a purpose for reading).

7. Tell students that during reading, they should be looking for the answers to their questions. Read the book aloud to the class.

8. Return to the chart to list "What We Learned" and also "What We Still Wonder." Follow the procedure described in Steps 4 and 5 and have students post their notes in the correct columns. If questions in the "What We Want to Learn" column have been answered, move those notes to the "What We Learned" column." You may want to jot a brief answer on them.

Section Seven

Summarizing

Summarizing is a far more sophisticated task than it first might appear to experienced readers. All too often summarizing is confused with merely choosing what is most important in text, but genuine summarizing goes far beyond that simple activity (Dole, Duffy, Roehler, and Pearson, 1991). The summarizing process actually calls on a number of higher-level thinking skills. To be able to create a summary, you must "discern the most central and important ideas in the text . . . generalize from examples or from things that are repeated . . . and ignore irrelevant details" (NRPR, 2000). The reader must not only separate what is most important from what is of lesser importance but must also synthesize the prioritized information to form a new text, of sorts, that stands for the original text. A pretty tall order for a first grader!

However, if we do it appropriately by setting a foundation and then slowly introducing the concept, teaching our youngest readers about summarizing is not only possible—it's definitely worth the effort. In fact, for a number of reasons, summarizing improves overall comprehension of text (Duke, Pearson, 2003). For example, summarizing can improve memory for what is read, both in terms of free recall and answering questions (NRPR, 2000).

With the distinct benefits of teaching children to summarize in mind, we must also understand what research says is necessary for this learning to take place. Many, if not most, children require direct instruction in the different skills and sub-tasks involved in summarizing. The teacher's role is critical in explaining what must occur and in modeling how the process looks and sounds. Further, in order to produce good oral and written summaries of text, students must have adequate time for applying what they've learned and for practicing summarizing. With instruction and practice, not only will they become better at summarizing, they'll become better readers (Pearson, Duke, 2003).

As you'll see from the range of lessons in this section, summarization can take many different forms. After the first lesson, which lays key groundwork by helping students retell what they've read, the activities branch out in varied directions. In several creative ways—including dramatics and drawing—students learn to home in on key information, condensing and interpreting what is most important in a text. For narrative text, students are introduced to the story structure of beginning, middle, and end; for expository text, they learn a different kind of organization—topic, main idea, and supporting details. Each provides a logical base for summarizing key information in that genre. Other fun activities involve using a special alphabet chart to record key words or writing captions for artwork. Overall, the lessons move from working at the word level to the big picture—from part to whole—to get at the heart of what is being read.

Capturing the essence of a reading selection . . . this is what summarizing is all about. Simple on the surface, yet quite a sophisticated task after all!

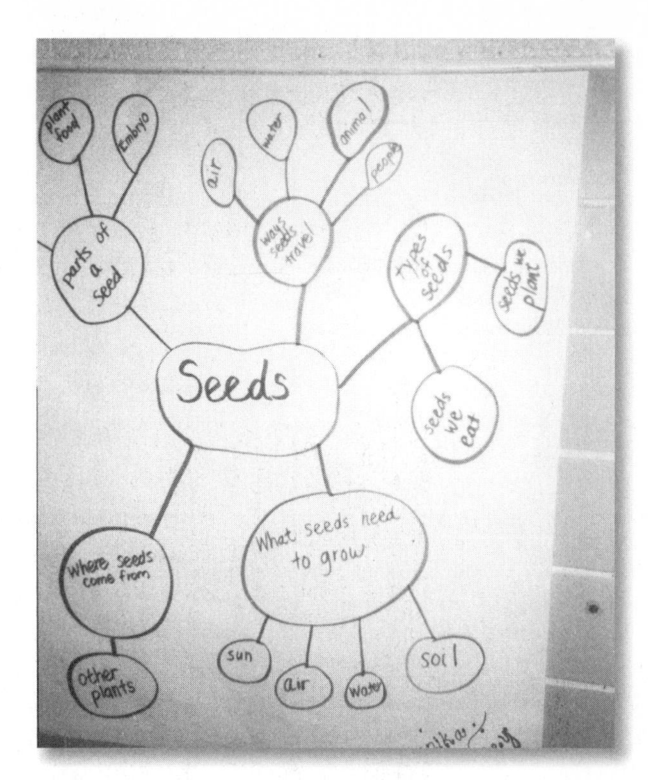

This topic, or bubble, map helps students to see the relationships among ideas in the science text they're reading.

Details	Details	Details	Details	Details
Thin legs	flies	red with black spots	digs	can sting
Spins Webs	thin and flat	Walking around on her hand	Six legs	Buzzes
fat	Sips from flowers	Wings	Small	

Based on their reading, one class is creating a matrix to compare and contrast information about five different bugs.

STORY BITS

Explanation

This lesson emphasizes fundamental skills of retelling and recalling as it helps prepare students to launch into the complex skill of summarizing. Students are given a concrete reminder to help them retell a story and/or recall facts from a book they have just heard or read. You might adopt this activity as a regular part of your weekly plan—it is a great way of creating a connection between home and school. So often, children don't relay anything specific about what they've learned in school. Their special mementos will remind them of what they can share.

Skill Focus

Retelling stories; recalling details in texts; responding to text in a variety of ways; developing vocabulary through meaningful/concrete experiences

Materials & Resources

Text

- Any grade-appropriate fiction or nonfiction text (Used in this lesson: *Tell Me Why Rain Is Wet* by Shirley Willis)

Other

- For each student: a cotton ball representing a cloud (or another small memento to remind students about the text) and, if this activity is used regularly, a sealable plastic bag or a pencil box for storing their collections of story bits

STEPS

1. Tell students that good readers know it is very important to remember what they have read. Being able to recall facts or retell a story are some ways readers show that they have remembered a text. Explain that you want students to read (or listen) very carefully to today's story because they'll be expected to retell what the book is about. To help them do this, you're going to give them something special. It will be a little reminder of what the book is about.

2. Read the selected text to or with your students. Hold up your own memento and model how you use it to help you remember. For example, with the sample text, you would hold up your "cloud" (a cotton ball) and say, "Boys and girls, this cloud reminds me that our book, *Tell Me Why Rain Is Wet*, is about rain. It tells us how the water gathers in the air around us and rises above us. The clouds are where the moisture comes together. When the clouds are too heavy with water, the drops begin to fall back to Earth. That's when we get rain, or sometimes snow or sleet. We learned about different kinds of clouds, too, and which ones we're likely to see if it's going to rain. Goodness! We learned a lot in this little book!"

3. Now give all students a "cloud" of their very own. Pair each child with a buddy and have them take turns telling what the book was about.

4. Tell students that you want them to take their clouds home tonight. They are to show the cotton ball to a family member and use it to help retell what they learned from today's book.

5. If you plan to use this activity regularly, distribute a sealable plastic bag or pencil box to each student. Have them bring home the "cloud" in the bag or box and return with it the next day.

6. This is an excellent ongoing, school-year-long activity. Occasionally, allow time for students to sit with a friend, or even alone, to go back through their collection of bits to remember what they've read this year. You may also want to send these bits home regularly (in their protective bags or boxes) so that students can be reminded of stories to retell to their parents.

USING DRAMA TO SUMMARIZE MAIN EVENTS IN NARRATIVE TEXT

Explanation

Drama is a great way for young children to express themselves. In this lesson, at the same time that students are having fun acting, they are learning to process text structure in terms of beginning, middle, and end. As they do so, they are also learning to summarize text events (although that concept is only referred to by name very briefly in this introductory lesson).

Skill Focus

Retelling stories; recalling information from text; responding to text through creative dramatics; recognizing the beginning, middle, and end of a story

Materials & Resources

Text

- Any grade-appropriate narrative text with simple plot development (Used in this lesson: *Flower Garden* by Eve Bunting)

Bonus Ideas

As you encourage drama in your classroom, don't forget how valuable paper grocery bags can be. You might want to ask parents to save their paper bags for this purpose. Add a little color, snip here and there–and you have quick and easy costumes and masks!

STEPS

1. Tell students that one way good readers understand and remember a story better is by thinking about the events that happen in the beginning, the middle, and the end of a story. In today's lesson, students are going to focus on these events, but they're going to do this in a very special way. They're going to have a chance to be actors and to act out a story!

2. Read aloud the selected story just for enjoyment. Then tell students that you want them to pay close attention to the sequence of the events—what happens first, next, and last—and read the story a second time.

3. Call on students to help you list briefly what happened in the beginning, middle, and end of the story. Record their responses on the board or on a transparency. For the sample story, a summary might look like this:

Beginning	Middle	End
Girl goes to the store. She gets a shopping cart and buys plants and supplies. She goes through the checkout to pay. The girl and her dad go home on the bus.	They get home and go upstairs. They spread out newspapers and plant a garden in a box. The flowers go on the windowsill. They light candles on a cake.	Mom comes home and has a big birthday surprise!

4. Organize students into three groups. Assign each group to be the beginning, the middle, or the end of the story. (If you have too many students to work well in only three groups, you might want to set up two sets of three groups. Each set will have its own beginning, middle, and end group and will give its own performance.) Instruct students to refer to the notes that the class has made on the chart and to discuss how they will act out their assigned part of the plot. Circulate among the groups, offering guidance and helping students choose roles and create brief dialogue.

5. When students have had adequate time, settle the class comfortably so that they can enjoy the production. Announce the title and author of the story. Have the first group stand and offer their interpretation of what happened in the beginning of the story. Group two follows with the middle, and group three with the end.

6. When all groups have performed, discuss with the class how their acting has retold, or summarized, the main events of the story. As you use the term *summarized*, tell students that they will learn more about this new term and this skill in the next lesson.

MINI-LESSON

TWO-PART LESSON: BEGINNING, MIDDLE, AND END FLIP BOOK

PART 1: USING THE FLIP BOOK TO SUMMARIZE WITH PICTURES

Explanation

After a couple of introductory lessons, students are now ready for you to introduce the concept of summary. This two-part lesson teaches that concept while continuing to focus on the major beginning, middle, and ending events of a narrative text. In this first part of the lesson, students create Flip Books and depict major events through illustrations.

Skill Focus

Retelling stories; recalling information from text; responding to texts graphically and verbally; recognizing the beginning, middle, and end of a story; summarizing main ideas

Materials & Resources

Text

- Grade-appropriate narrative texts with simple plot development (Used in this lesson: *The Mysterious Tadpole* by Steven Kellogg)

Other

- Scissors
- Pencils/crayons
- For each student: 1 sheet of unlined paper

Prior to the Lesson: *To create a model Flip Book, fold a piece of paper in half lengthwise. Cut two slits into the paper at $1/3$ and at $2/3$ of the length from the outside edge to the middle fold. In the top rows, write "beginning," "middle," and "end."*

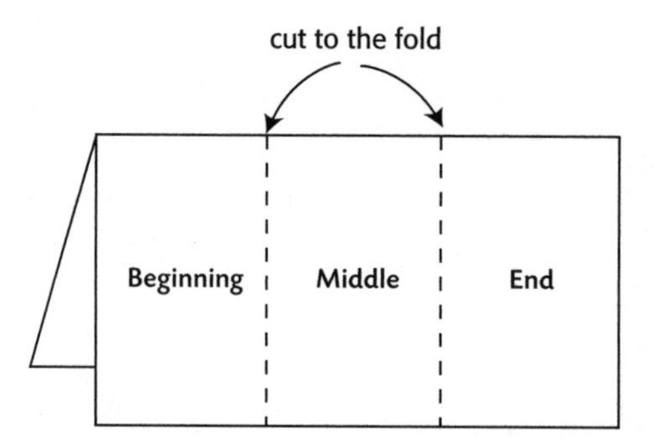

STEPS

1. Explain to students that summarizing means focusing on the important facts or events in a text and being able to recall and retell that information. To help students grasp the concept of summary, present a graphic example like the one below:

$$\begin{array}{r} 2 \\ 3 \\ 1 \\ +\,4 \\ \hline 10 \end{array}$$

   Circle the "sum" and explain that the sum is all of the numbers added together. The sum is the shortest way of writing all the numbers. Write the word *summary*, and underline the word part *sum*. Inform students that they'll be summarizing in two different ways today—by illustrating and by telling.

2. Remind students that although stories typically include many different events, they can usually be summarized in three segments—beginning, middle, and end. Read a short narrative text to or with students. Instruct them to listen carefully for the major events in the beginning, middle, and end.

3. Model how you summarize this story's events in your Flip Book. Reread the beginning of the text. Think aloud about the most important idea and show students how you sketch out a quick picture of that idea under the word *beginning*. When you've finished drawing, demonstrate how the Flip Book works: you can flip up the word *beginning* to reveal the picture.

4. Follow the same procedure for the middle and the end of the story. The chart below describes the pictures you might create for the sample book:

Beginning	Middle	End
[Your drawing of a boy with a box that is labeled "tadpole"]	[Your drawing of the boy standing beside the monster into which the tadpole has grown]	[Your drawing of the boy and the monster swimming happily in a lake]

5. Distribute materials to students and instruct them to make their own Flip Books, following your model. Circulate among them, offering guidance and help as necessary.

6. Conclude the lesson by having students read either an assigned or an independent narrative story and drawing their own Flip Book illustrations. Tell them that in the next part of this lesson, they'll have a chance to use words to describe the same events.

TWO-PART LESSON: BEGINNING, MIDDLE, AND END FLIP BOOK

PART 2: USING THE FLIP BOOK TO SUMMARIZE WITH WORDS

Explanation

The second part of this lesson continues to focus on the concept of summarizing by emphasizing the major events at the beginning, middle, and end of a narrative text. Here students complete their Flip Books by adding words to their illustrations so that in the end they have created both visual and verbal summaries of a story.

Skill Focus

Retelling stories; recalling information from text; responding to texts graphically and verbally; recognizing the beginning, middle, and end of a story; summarizing main ideas

Materials & Resources

Text

- Same narrative text used in Part 1 of this lesson (Used in this lesson: *The Mysterious Tadpole* by Steven Kellogg)

Other

- Flip Books from Part 1 of this lesson

Bonus Ideas

The Flip Book has multiple uses: 1) draw characters on the flaps and jot clues/descriptions about them underneath; 2) write vocabulary words on top and define or illustrate them underneath; 3) write a math problem on the flap and explain it underneath. The possibilities are endless!

STEPS

1. Display your Flip Book from Part 1 of this lesson. Remind students that so far you have summarized the beginning, middle, and end of the story with illustrations that show those three major events. Explain that today you're going to complete your Flip Book by using words to summarize the same events.

2. Quickly review the three important ideas you've summarized in your drawings. Think aloud about ways you might describe those same events. After deciding on the best way to express each of the three segments, add your comments to your Flip Book. The chart below shows wordings you might use for the sample book:

Beginning	Middle	End
[Words to go with the drawing:] "The boy in the story gets a present of a tadpole from his uncle in Scotland."	[Words to go with the drawing:] "The tadpole grows into a big monster and the boy has trouble taking care of it."	[Words to go with the drawing:] "It turns out the tadpole is from the Loch Ness Monster in Scotland! The boy finds a way to take care of him, though!"

3. Distribute to each student his or her own Flip Book from Part 1 of this lesson. Challenge them to use their verbal skills to summarize the same beginning, middle, and end story events that they've already illustrated. Circulate among students, offering guidance and help as necessary.

SUMMARIZING INFORMATIONAL TEXT

Explanation

This lesson allows students to experience how expository text structure is different from narrative text. Students summarize informational text first by identifying an umbrella topic, then by using pictures to capture key details, and finally by using those drawings to express the main idea of the text.

Skill Focus

Retelling stories; identifying topic, main idea, and supporting details in informational text; summarizing main ideas

Materials & Resources

Text

- A brief informational piece without subheadings (Used in this lesson: spider information at enchantedlearning.com)

Other

- Transparency of Informational Text Chart (see App., p. 125)
- For each student: 1 photocopy of same chart

Bonus Ideas

Have students complete the Informational Text Chart for independent reading books. Invite them to sit with partners to retell what they've included on their charts. Have them use this outline to help them structure their retellings:

- I read about (Topic).
- The author said these things: (Box 1, Box 2, Box 3, Box 4).
- I think the author wrote this to tell me (Main Idea).

STEPS

1. Remind students that it's important for them to be able to retell the main points—to summarize—what they read. Briefly review their experiences summarizing narrative texts in previous lessons. Tell students that today they'll practice summarizing informational text.

2. Display the transparency of the Informational Text Chart and point to each section as you explain to students that nonfiction text is created, or structured, differently from narrative text. It does not have beginning, middle, and end events. Instead, it has a topic, which is the big subject it's about, and it has a main idea, which tells us the most important idea we need to remember. It also has factual details that give more information about the main idea.

3. Read the selected text to or with the class.

4. Discuss how a reader might identify the topic of the text. For example, with the sample text, you might discuss that since the whole article is about how spiders eat, how they spin silk, and where they live, the topic for this text could be summed up in one word: *spiders*. (Be sure to explain that sometimes it takes more than one word to express a topic.)

5. Now distribute a photocopy of the chart to each student. Have students write the agreed-upon topic on the top line as you fill in the same word(s) on the transparency.

6. Discuss with students that the article has stated many interesting facts about the topic. Help the class cull some of the most relevant or informative details from the article. Guide them to illustrate four of those points within the four large quadrants on their charts. Sketch in your own illustrations on the transparency. For the sample text, for example, the four sketches might illustrate these points:
   - Spiders sometimes eat each other.
   - Spiders use silk to make webs and traps.
   - When adjusted for weight, the spider's silk is stronger than steel.
   - The female spider's egg sac can contain up to 1,000 eggs.

7. Next, focus on the oval in the middle of the chart. Draw students' attention to the term "Main Idea." Work with the class to come up with one sentence that answers this question: "What did all four points together tell the reader?" For the sample text, for example, the main idea might be:
   - Spiders are truly amazing creatures!

TWO-PART LESSON: IDENTIFYING KEY WORDS IN TEXT FOR SUMMARIZING

PART 1: FINDING AND RECORDING THE KEY WORDS

Explanation

This lesson is more difficult than it appears. It calls on several higher-level thought processes as it requires students to read, separate key words from the main text, and locate appropriate alphabetical spots for recording the words. They'll enjoy doing this, though—the chart is a bit like a game board that they can have fun filling in!

Skill Focus

Recalling information from text; summarizing main ideas; using alphabetical order to locate information

Materials & Resources

Text

- Any grade-appropriate informational text (Used in this lesson: *Bear Facts* by Gare Thompson)

Other

- Laminated poster board of the Alpha-Key Words Chart (see Appendix, p. 126) or transparency of the same chart
- Marker; narrow tape (optional)
- For each student: 1 photocopy of the Alpha-Key Words Chart (optional)

Bonus Ideas

You might also use these charts to help develop good listening skills. Give students a copy of the chart and instruct them to record key words from a discussion or a read-aloud.

Prior to the Lesson: *Because it will provide year-round use, we recommend creating a large, laminated version of the Alpha-Key Words chart. If you choose to do this, use the Appendix on page 126 as a template and, either with marker or with narrow, colored tape, mark off the cells and then write the letters and the word* Topic *as shown. Be sure to laminate your poster so that you can use it repeatedly. If you prefer, simply make a transparency of the Appendix chart for this lesson.*

STEPS

1. Tell students that good readers look for key words in text. These important words help them remember, summarize, and retell what they've read and learned. Let students know that in today's lesson they will work with a special chart to help them find and record key words.

2. Display and discuss the Alpha Key-Words Chart, as a poster-board chart or on a transparency. Read a page of your selected text and model for students how you use the chart to record key words. For example, for the sample text, after the first page, you might say, "This page is about black bears, so I'm going to write *black bears* in the square for B's. The book makes a point that they are big, so I'll write the word *big*, too." Proceed in a similar way through the next several pages, thinking aloud as you select and record words. Be sure to tell students that because you're selecting only key words, many chart cells will not be filled. To underscore this point, explain that if every letter of the alphabet were represented, there would be unimportant words that would not help with summarizing key points.

3. After a few pages of modeling how to use the chart, invite students to join in. You might have them read with you as you gather the remaining words together. Alternately, you might distribute photocopies of the chart to each student and direct them to work with a partner or in a small group. A partially completed chart for the sample book might look like this:

Alpha-Key Words Chart

A	B black bears big	C climbers cubs	D	E	F fishers
G	H	Topic Bears		I	J
K	L			M mother bears	N
O	P polar bears	Q	R	S swimmers	T
U	V	W	X	Y	Z

4. Conclude the lesson by reminding students that they will be putting these charts to good use tomorrow as they write factual summaries.

TWO-PART LESSON: IDENTIFYING KEY WORDS IN TEXT FOR SUMMARIZING

PART 2: WRITING THE SUMMARY

Explanation

In this second part of the lesson, students take their Alpha-Key Words Charts one step further. They learn to use the words they've gathered to write a summary of the important facts or events in the reading selection.

Skill Focus

Recalling information from text; summarizing main ideas; using alphabetical order to locate information

Materials & Resources

Text

- Same informational text used in Part 1 of this lesson (Used in this lesson: *Bear Facts* by Gare Thompson)

Other

- Laminated poster board of Alpha-Key Words Chart or transparency from Part 1 of this lesson
- Marker
- If used in Part 1, students' copies of the Alpha-Key Words Chart

Bonus Ideas

You might also use Alpha-Key Words Charts for students to collect topics for their own writing. Take out the charts periodically and brainstorm topics and related words that the class has learned. Record those and keep the charts available for students to search through for potential ideas for their writing.

STEPS

1. Review the purpose of the Alpha-Key Words Chart, presented in the previous lesson. Remind students that this chart has helped the class choose words in the text that are important to comprehend the material. Today they are going to work with those words to create a summary of the text.

2. Instruct students to listen carefully as you read the text again. You want them to decide if any words should have been included that were not. You also want them to check for any unimportant words that might have been included but that don't really belong on the chart.

3. Reread the text, discussing and clarifying words as you proceed. Cross out words that the class decides aren't necessary and add those that are. Guide students as necessary to make accurate choices.

4. Note that if students have filled in their own Alpha-Key Words Charts in the previous lesson, distribute these so that students can refer to them as well as to the whole-class chart during Steps 2 and 3. In the end, all the charts should read the same.

5. Tell students that the next step is to use the chart words to summarize what the text is about. (If necessary, review the definition of summarizing: retelling in a brief way the most important events or facts in a text.) Explain that you're going to use the key words as the main ideas of the summary but that in order to write a good summary, you're going to need additional, connecting words. You might illustrate this by making a few random dots on the board. Tell students that the key words they've gathered are like these dots. When we summarize or retell, we have to connect the dots to express the ideas. Draw lines from one dot to another to show how the words will be connected.

6. Together with the class, create a summary based on the final charts. Call special attention to the key words and point out, too, the connecting words you need. A possible summary for the sample text might read as follows:

   Black bears are big. They are good climbers. Polar bears are even bigger. They are good swimmers. Brown bears are the biggest. They are good fishers. Mother bears are bigger than their cubs.

CAPTURING WITH CAPTIONS AND ILLUSTRATIONS

Explanation

This lesson picks up on the earlier Flip Book lessons and moves students from narrative to expository text. By teaching students to express main ideas through illustrations and captions, we encourage them to attend more closely to graphics in reading materials and enable them to express main ideas in nonverbal ways. In addition, drawing provides them with a more concrete means of capturing what can often be fairly abstract main ideas.

Skill Focus

Recalling information from text; summarizing main ideas; responding to text graphically and verbally

Materials & Resources

Text

- Any grade-appropriate informational text (Used in this lesson: *Flies for Dinner* by Robert Collins)

Other

- Several sheets of chart paper, a transparency, or a chalkboard

Bonus Ideas

For a great literacy center activity, find interesting pictures in magazines. Cut them out, glue them to white or pastel construction paper, and laminate them. Place transparency pens on a table with the pictures and allow students to write captions on the pictures. After reviewing them, erase the captions so that other students can have a turn.

STEPS

1. Review with students that there are many different ways good readers use to summarize text. In today's lesson, students will get a chance to put to use two of these ways as they capture the key ideas in an informational text selection.

2. Explain that you're going to read a section of text to them. Their task will be to listen carefully and to think of a way to illustrate the author's main point in that section.

3. Start by modeling the process. Read aloud a brief section of text and think aloud as you figure out its main point(s). Once you've identified the major idea in that section, sketch out a picture of what you've learned. You might allow students to make suggestions about how the picture should look.

4. Next, tell students that you need to create an explanation in words for that picture. Inform them that this kind of explanation is called a caption. Think aloud as you come up with a dozen or fewer words that describe the main idea depicted in your drawing. Write the caption directly under the drawing. For example, for the sample book, a picture and caption might look like this:

Many living things eat flies for dinner.

5. Now, read another chunk of text. This time, encourage a class discussion to come up with an image that summarizes the text.

6. Invite a volunteer to come forward and draw a picture to represent this image. Work together with the class to create an appropriate caption for the picture and either write it yourself or have a different volunteer come forward to write it.

7. Conclude by emphasizing that the picture summarizes the text's main idea and, in turn, the caption is a one-line summary of what the picture shows.

SUMMARIZING CHARACTERS FROM LITERAL AND INFERENTIAL INFORMATION

Explanation

First graders aren't too young to learn the difference between "finding out" (literal reading) and "figuring out" (inferential reading). Their initial preference may be to point to answers directly in the text, but they are really quite willing to think hard to make deeper sense of the text. This lesson not only teaches the difference between the two kinds of text information, but it provides a framework for students to compose a summary based on both kinds of information.

Skill Focus

Recalling information from text; summarizing main ideas; drawing conclusions and making inferences; analyzing characters

Materials & Resources

Text

- Any grade-appropriate narrative text with a strong main character (Used in this lesson: *My Special Day at Third Street School* by Eve Bunting)

Other

- Transparency or chalkboard

STEPS

1. Tell students that at the conclusion of today's lesson, they'll help you write a summary of a story's main character. First, however, they'll learn two different ways to get information from the story about this character.

2. Explain that authors often tell their readers specific information and facts about a character (or event). These are things we can point to, or "find out," right there in the text. But authors don't tell their readers everything. Sometimes readers have to use text clues and think hard, or "figure out," in order to discover information. To write the summary today, students will need to use both their finding out skills and their figuring out skills.

3. Read the story to or with students, just for enjoyment. Then go back through the story as a class, guiding students to examine all statements about and allusions to the character. On a transparency or the chalkboard, make a simple chart to record the information students uncover. For each fact, discuss whether the author stated that information outright or provided a clue. Help students discern the difference as you fill in the chart. A chart for the sample book might look like this:

Character: Miss Amanda Drake

What do we know about this character?	Does the author tell us this or give us a clue?	What was the clue?
She's an author.	Tells us	
She has written lots of books.	Tells us	
She is tall and thin with pink-streaked hair.	Tells us	
She loves animals of all kinds.	Gives us clues	She cuddles all of the class animals. She holds the snake. She says she has a rat.
She's really nice and likes kids.	Gives us clues	She kicks the spilled ice and gives the boy a wink. She writes to children. She writes a book about them.

4. Conclude the lesson by having students work together to create a summary paragraph of the important information they learned about the character. A sample paragraph follows:

Amanda Drake is an author who has written a lot of books. She is tall and thin with pink-streaked hair. She's a really nice person. She loves all kinds of animals and she likes children.

Section Eight

Using Text Features and Organizers

The manner in which text is organized, arranged, and presented to the reader is far from arbitrary. Especially in informational text, but in drama, poetry, and fiction as well, authors and editors purposefully include elements to help readers navigate texts. Too often, however, students of all ages overlook even obvious text signals. As teachers we can address this situation by providing effective direct instruction in how to use these kinds of features.

Potentially helpful text signals abound. Books are divided into logical sections to help readers focus on specifics. Tables of contents and indexes help readers locate those specifics more efficiently so that they do not have to wade through pages of irrelevant material. Chapters, headings, and subheadings are provided to categorize and prioritize material. Special effects—such as boldfaced or italicized words, photo captions, or sidebar boxes—are also used to enhance presentation of important material.

In this section, you'll find lessons that focus on the text features and organizers most helpful and appropriate for first graders. We start with true basics—identification of author and illustrator—and move from there to work with book parts such as tables of contents and glossaries. Because students' learning can be strengthened by active participation, we not only model the use of these features, we also engage students in creating class books that include various book parts. Other lessons focus on highlighted special words and on headings and subheadings. The section also includes a lesson that tackles text signals from a somewhat different angle—an internal text structure (sequencing) that is indicated by specific word clues. The two concluding lessons introduce students to the genres of poetry and drama by spotlighting both external and internal text features.

Our goal throughout is to help students improve their reading and understanding by giving them a better grasp of the uniqueness of the many text structures and signals that are there to help them. We cannot assume that they will see the obvious. Our job, as in so much of education, is to help them find the way.

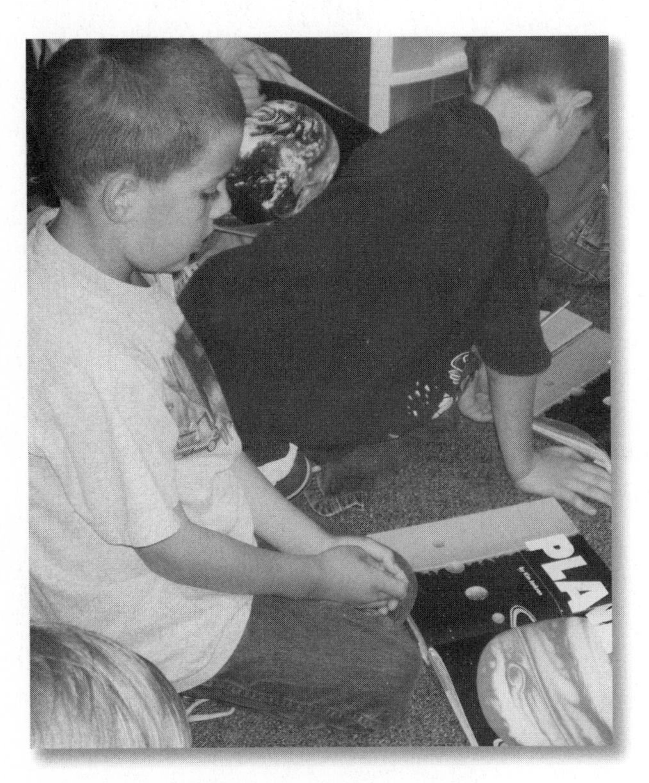

These boys use a table of contents and chapter headings to locate information in a science text.

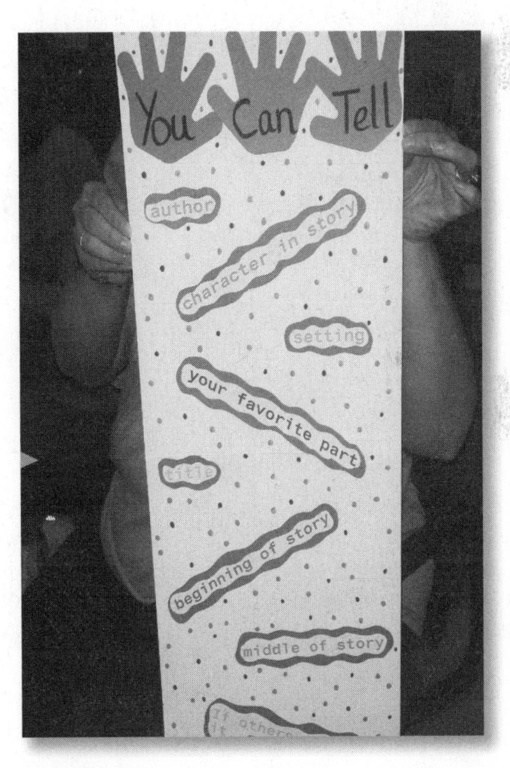

This chart helps students understand narrative text structure.

WHAT'S IN A NAME? THE AUTHOR

Explanation

There are so many wonderful authors and illustrators you'll want to acquaint your students with during the school year. Students must learn to identify the name of the author and illustrator and understand the roles they play. Identification, however, is only a first step. Students should come to know and appreciate the authors and illustrators who bring such talent to the text page. This lesson will help you accomplish just that!

Skill Focus

Using text features/organizers to obtain information; identifying title, author, and illustrator of a text as well as parts of a book; responding to texts through writing and art; identifying genre characteristics

Materials & Resources

Text

- Any grade-appropriate fiction or nonfiction book (perhaps one that is already familiar to the class) by an author whom you're likely to read often during the year (Used in this lesson: *Today I Feel Silly & Other Moods That Make My Day* by Jamie Lee Curtis)

Other

- A sheet of white or pastel poster board
- Colored markers
- Three 2" silver clasp rings
- Hole puncher

Prior to the Lesson: *Cut the poster board in half widthwise. Hole-punch three holes in the left margin of the longest sides of each half and connect the two sheets with the clasp rings.*

STEPS

1. Let students know that today they'll begin to make a resource for the classroom. Explain that together you're going to start a book about the people who've written the books students will be reading this year.
2. Gather students around you and display the poster-board book. Write the word *Authors* on the front page. Tell students that *author* is the special name given to the people who write books.
3. Now add to the title so that the final version reads: "Authors We Love!" Tell students that when the class finds a favorite author—one whom they really love—this book will be the place to write about that author. They will add a new page to the book just for that author; this will give them a special way to remember their favorites. You might let them know that their book will be a good resource for next year's first-grade class, too!
4. If you wish, provide crayons and markers and invite volunteers to come forward to decorate the cover page. Otherwise, set aside a later time for this activity.
5. Now flip to the second page of the "Authors" book. As students watch, create a template for this page by writing in the following headings in the left-hand column: "Author," "Books by This Author," "Topics of These Books," "Something About the Author," and "What We Like Best."
6. Display the book you've selected. Read it to or with your students. (This might be a book that is already a favorite in your class.)
7. After the reading, invite students to help you fill in information on the author page. See page 104 for an example page, based on the sample book.
8. Choose a prominent place in the classroom to display the new book. Be prepared to add new pages as your class discovers new favorite authors!

WHAT'S IN A NAME? THE ILLUSTRATOR

Explanation

Just as you've created your "Authors We Love!" class book, you'll want to create an "Illustrators We Love!" book to celebrate the wonderful artists who have illustrated favorite books the class is reading this year. This lesson gives students the chance to start this second classroom resource book, surely one that they'll look forward to augmenting all year long.

Skill Focus

Using text features/organizers to obtain information; identifying title, author, and illustrator of a text as well as parts of a book; responding to texts through writing and art; identifying genre characteristics

Materials & Resources

Text

- Any grade-appropriate fiction or nonfiction book (perhaps one that is already familiar to the class) with an illustrator whose art you're likely to enjoy often (Used in this lesson: *Kitten's First Full Moon*, written and illustrated by Kevin Henkes)

Other

- A sheet of white or pastel poster board
- Colored markers; hole puncher
- Three 2" silver clasp rings

Bonus Ideas

Continue to add new pages when you or your students find artists you think are special. Use this as a reference book and to compare and contrast artists' styles.

Prior to the Lesson: *Cut the poster board in half widthwise. Hole-punch three holes in the left margin of the longest sides of each half and connect the two sheets with the clasp rings.*

STEPS

1. Let students know that just as they made a favorite authors book, today they'll begin to create another classroom resource—this time a book that records information about favorite illustrators and their books.
2. Gather students around you and display the poster-board book. Write the word *Illustrators* on the front page. Explain that illustrators are the artists who draw the pictures in the books they read. Illustrations help bring words to life.
3. Now add to the title so that the final version reads: "Illustrators We Love!" Tell students that when the class finds a favorite illustrator—one whom they really love—this book will be the place to write about that artist. They will add a new page to the book just for that illustrator; this will give them a special way to remember their favorites. You might let them know that their book will be a good resource for next year's first-grade class, too!
4. If you wish, provide crayons and markers and invite volunteers to come forward to decorate the cover page. Otherwise, set aside a later time for this activity. Whenever you do it, encourage students to be creative, as that will make them feel like authors and illustrators, too!
5. Now flip to the second page of the "Illustrators" book. As students watch, create a template for this page by writing in the following headings in the left-hand column: "Illustrator," "Books by This Illustrator," "Topics of These Books," "Something About the Illustrator," and "What We Like Best."
6. Display the book you've selected. Read it to or with your students. (This might be a book that is already a favorite in your class and/or a book that has been recognized for its art.) After reading the book once, go back through, calling attention to the artwork. For example, for the sample book, you might make specific comments like, "These drawings are only in black, gray, and white, but they're so pretty," or "I love the way the illustrator makes the lightning bugs look like they're really shining in these pictures!"
7. After the reading, invite students to help you fill in information on the illustrator page. See page 104 for an example page, based on the sample book.

SAMPLE PAGE FOR "AUTHORS" BOOK

Author:	**Jamie Lee Curtis**
Books by This Author:	*Today I Feel Silly & Other Moods That Make My Day* *Where Do Balloons Go? An Uplifting Mystery* *When I Was Little: A Four-Year-Old's Memoir of Her Youth*
Topics or Themes of These Books:	Feelings Balloons Memories
Something About the Author:	She's a movie star.
What We Like Best:	She makes funny rhymes. There's a turning wheel in one book.

SAMPLE PAGE FOR "ILLUSTRATORS" BOOK

Illustrator:	**Kevin Henkes**
Books by This Illustrator:	*Kitten's First Full Moon* *Lilly's Purple Plastic Purse* *Owen* *Chrysanthemum*
Topics or Themes of These Books:	Cat confuses the full moon for milk. Lilly the mouse learns a lesson about bad behavior. Owen the mouse learns a clever way to give up his baby blanket.
Something About the Illustrator:	He is also an author. He won a Caldecott Award. He lives in Madison, Wisconsin.
What We Like Best:	He can make drawings pretty without bright colors. He uses big and small drawings. His drawings look simple. The animals look like they have real feelings.

FOUR-PART LESSON: PARTS OF A BOOK—TABLE OF CONTENTS

PART 1: LEARNING ABOUT A TABLE OF CONTENTS

Explanation

Students need to understand that the different parts of a book are there to help them read and study. Even young readers can learn not only to identify the parts of books but also to begin to put them to use. In this first part of a series of lessons, students learn how a book's table of contents can help them preview and locate information.

Skill Focus

Using text features/organizers to obtain information; identifying title, author, and illustrator of a text as well as parts of a book; identifying genre characteristics; categorizing and classifying words and ideas

Materials & Resources

Text

- An informational book with a table of contents (Used in this lesson: *A Look at Spiders* by Jerald Halpern)
- Additional informational books with tables of contents (either multiple copies of same book or different books)

Other

- A sticky note for each partner group of students
- A bag or sack containing miscellaneous small items such as erasers, rubber bands, and beads

STEPS

1. Explain that books are made up of different important parts. Good readers look for these parts to help them read and study. Tell students that they will be learning about a few key parts to watch out for. The first part appears in the beginning of the book and is called the *table of contents.* It helps readers preview a book so that they will have a better idea of what to expect inside the book. It also helps readers locate information quickly so that they don't have to look all the way through the book to find something. Discuss the word *table* with the class. Explain that it has multiple meanings. This one isn't the place on which we eat our dinner! Sometimes a table is a graph or chart. Sometimes it is an organized listing. That's the meaning that applies to books.

2. Now discuss the word *contents*, which means "things that are included inside something else." Show them the bag or sack you have filled with small items. Invite volunteers to reach inside to find out what the "contents" are. Stress that a book's table of contents lists what you'll expect to find filling that book.

   Use the model book to examine a table of contents. For example, for the sample book, you might say, "What if I were curious about what spiders eat and wanted to read about it? I might not have time to read this whole book. I would open the book to the table of contents and read the different headings to see if I could locate something about spiders eating. Help me figure out where I need to turn. I'll read the headings. Give me a 'thumbs-up' if you think I should go to that section of the book to read. Or give me a 'thumbs-down' if you think that section won't have any information about what spiders eat." Here are the headings you would read for the sample book:

What Is a Spider?	How Big Are Spiders?
Where Do Spiders Live?	How Do Spiders Eat?

1. When students give the thumbs-up (as they should for the final heading in the list above), stop and turn to the indicated page number. Read a sufficient amount of text to confirm the selection. Be sure students realize that only the first page of a section is given in the table of contents. They may have to read past this page for the information they're looking for.

2. Set up partners. Distribute the additional text(s) to each pair and pose a question about the main topic. Instruct them to read the table of contents to find out which chapter would provide the appropriate information. Have pairs write on a sticky note the correct page they would turn to. Bring the class together to confirm what was correct and how they located it.

FOUR-PART LESSON: PARTS OF A BOOK—TABLE OF CONTENTS

PART 2: CREATING A TABLE OF CONTENTS

Explanation

What better way to teach children about the parts of a book than to get them to create those parts! This lesson takes off from the previous lesson: students put their new knowledge of tables of contents to use as they make a table of contents for their classroom Authors or Illustrators books.

Skill Focus

Using text features/organizers to obtain information; identifying title, author, and illustrator of a text as well as parts of a book; categorizing and classifying words and ideas

Materials & Resources

Text

- Any grade-appropriate book with a table of contents

Other

- The "Authors We Love!" book constructed in an earlier lesson (page 102) (Note: Although this lesson targets the Authors book, you might choose instead to use the Illustrators book)
- ½ sheet of poster board cut to match the existing pages of your class "Authors We Love!" book
- Colored markers; hole puncher

Bonus Ideas

Invite students to create a table of contents for the class book that you did not target in this lesson (that is, for the Illustrators book if you focused on the Authors book here, and vice versa).

Note: *This lesson works best if you have already completed about three or four author pages for your class book.*

STEPS

1. Remind students that books have important parts that can be useful to them as they read and study; briefly review the nature and characteristics of a table of contents. Tell students that today they'll help you make an important book part for the Authors book the class has already constructed. Point out that since you'll be adding many authors to this book throughout the year, it will become difficult to locate a particular author. Suggest something like, "Let's make a table of contents for our book today so that it will be much easier to use!"

2. Display a book with a table of contents. Refer to this as needed during the lesson so that students have a model available as they create their own table of contents.

3. Write "Table of Contents" at the top of the ½ sheet of poster board.

4. Open your "Authors We Love!" book and turn to the pages you've already created. Write the name of the first author as the first listing on the table of contents page. Draw in a dotted line from the title to the right-hand column and write "page 1." List all other authors you've included thus far, with the appropriate page numbers. The first entries for a sample table of contents page are shown at right.

Table of Contents

5. Hole-punch your new page and, perhaps with students' help, add it to the front of the Authors book. Invite volunteers to come forward to demonstrate how to find an author that you name.

6. Continue to add listings to your table of contents each time you add a page to your book.

Four-Part Lesson: Parts of a Book—Glossary

Part 3: Learning About the Glossary

Explanation

In this lesson, the third in this series, students continue to learn about the different parts of a book that are there to help them read and study. Here the focus is on the end of a book–the glossary. As students learn about the nature of a glossary, they will also pick up some basics about examining word parts and writing definitions.

Skill Focus

Using text features/organizers to obtain information; identifying parts of a book; categorizing and classifying words and ideas; using resources to build on word meanings; using structural clues to decode words and make meaning

Materials & Resources

Text

- Any grade-appropriate book with key vocabulary highlighted in the text and listed in a glossary

Other

- A primary-grade dictionary

Bonus Ideas

Choose several words from one particular page of a glossary that all students have access to. Write the selected words on individual pieces of paper or index cards. Distribute them to students who enjoy acting. Offering your guidance as needed, have students study their word and its definition. Invite students to act out the word as all other students try to figure out what it is.

Note: *Before using this lesson, read through the lesson on page 109, paying particular attention to its Note.*

Steps

1. Display a copy of a primary-grade dictionary. Many students will, no doubt, be familiar with this resource. Discuss its nature and characteristics as well as how it is typically used.
2. Now write the word *dictionary* on the board, followed by this sentence:

   Dictionary: A dictionary tells what words mean.
3. Next, ask if your students know the word *vocabulary*. Again, they're likely to be familiar with this word. Call on volunteers to help you define the word. Conclude by writing on the board:

   Vocabulary: Vocabulary means words that help us understand.
4. Now underline the suffix *-ary* in *dictionary* and *vocabulary*. Mention that this word part indicates things that are connected. Underline, as well, the word *words* in each definitional sentence above. Explain that both the dictionary and vocabulary are "connected to words." (Keep this discussion simple—these are first graders! But most should be able to follow this basic introduction to these terms and concepts.)
5. Now write the word *glossary*. Ask if students notice something similar about this word. Guide them to conclude that it also has the *-ary* word part. Explain that many informational books have a glossary. You might let students guess what purpose a glossary serves. Help them to understand that a glossary also deals with words. Write this sentence:

   Glossary: A glossary tells us the important words in a book and what those words mean.
6. Underline the suffix *-ary* and the word *words* as you have done in the previous two sentences to help students grasp the links.
7. Finally, select a page in your sample book that contains a highlighted key word. Read the word aloud, then turn to the glossary. Show students how you find the word and check its definition. Sum up by saying something like, " A glossary serves as a dictionary of vocabulary words that are important in a book."

FOUR-PART LESSON: PARTS OF A BOOK—GLOSSARY

PART 4: CREATING A GLOSSARY

Explanation

Like the equivalent lesson on tables of contents (see page 106), this lesson offers a dynamic way to teach children about the parts of a book by involving them in creating those parts. Here students put their new knowledge of glossaries to use as they highlight key words in their class "Illustrators We Love!" (or "Authors We Love!") book and then make a glossary for those words.

Skill Focus

Using text features/organizers to obtain information; identifying parts of a book; categorizing and classifying words and ideas; using resources to build on word meanings; using content vocabulary

Materials & Resources

Text

- Any grade-appropriate book with key vocabulary highlighted in the text and listed in a glossary

Other

- The "Illustrators We Love!" book constructed in an earlier lesson (page 103) (Note: Although this lesson targets the Illustrators book, you might choose instead to use the Authors book)
- ½ sheet of poster board cut to match the existing pages of your class "Illustrators We Love!" book
- Colored markers
- Hole puncher

Note: *This lesson works best if you have already completed about three or four illustrator pages for your class book. Before using this lesson, read through the lesson on page 109, paying particular attention to its Note.*

STEPS

1. Briefly review the nature and characteristics of glossaries: they tell us the meanings of important, highlighted words in a book. Inform students that today they'll be adding a glossary page to their Illustrators book. Explain that since many of the informational pages will likely include specialized words, a glossary will be a very helpful addition for their book.

2. Display a book that uses underlining or colors to call attention to specialized vocabulary and important words and that contains a glossary. Refer to this as needed during the lesson so that students have a model available as they create their own glossary.

3. Open your "Illustrators We Love!" book to a page you've already created. Use a colored marker to highlight important words on that page. For example, in the sample Illustrators book in the lesson on page 103, you might highlight both the word *illustrator* and the term *Caldecott Award.*

4. Write "Glossary" at the top of the ½ sheet of poster board. Write your first key word to start the glossary page. Next to it include a simple definition for the word. Follow the same procedure—highlighting key words and terms and adding and defining them in the glossary—for all pages you've created thus far. The first entries for a sample glossary page are shown at right.

> **Glossary**
>
> (Page 1) **Illustrator:** The person who draws the pictures in the book.
>
> (Page 1) **Caldecott Award:** A prize given each year to the best art in a children's book in the United States.

5. You might explain to students that like dictionaries, most glossaries are alphabetized. But because the class is creating this one as they go along, it will be organized by the order of pages on which words occur.

6. Hole-punch your new page and add it to back of the Illustrators book. Invite volunteers to demonstrate how to locate and look up a key word.

7. As you add specialized vocabulary words to your book, underline them in the same color and add them, with definitions, to the glossary.

SPOTLIGHTING SPECIAL WORDS

Explanation

Like the lessons on glossaries, this lesson calls students' attention to highlighted words in texts. But here the focus is primarily on helping students notice the words and how they are spotlighted in text. Students learn how different books—and this is especially true of textbooks and basal program readers—highlight important words in a variety of ways.

Skill Focus

Using text features/organizers to obtain information; categorizing and classifying words and ideas; identifying and using content (specialized) vocabulary; developing vocabulary through meaningful/ concrete experiences

Materials & Resources

Text

- Several books with special vocabulary that is highlighted by boldfaced type, color, italics, or underlining

Other

- Sticky notes snipped into VIP strips (about 4 cuts to make 5 fingers; see page 12 for further information about VIP strips)

Bonus Ideas

To augment this lesson, after students have marked a text's highlighted words with their VIP strips, challenge them to write (right on the strips) synonyms and/or antonyms for those words. Or, provide students with the synonym/ antonym, have them write it on the strip, and then hunt for and flag the word it matches in the text.

Note: *This lesson works well in conjunction with the previous two lessons on glossaries. You can use it in several different ways—before those lessons to give students initial practice in work with highlighted words; along with those lessons to help students gain a tool for locating the words; or after the lessons for reinforcement in noticing these words.*

STEPS

1. Remind students that authors have a special way of calling attention to words that are important to readers. Discuss the various ways that key terms and vocabulary can be highlighted in books (especially informational books). Guide the discussion to include words highlighted in color, boldfaced words, italicized words, and underlined words. You might display an example of each on the board or a transparency. Explain that readers can usually skim a page with their eyes and immediately find those words.

2. Organize students in small groups of three to five. Distribute VIP strips to each group. Provide each group with a book that has specialized vocabulary notated in various ways. Tell students you'll set a timer for about three minutes. Their job is to use the VIP strips to mark words that have been called out in some way as important. When they find one, they should tear off a "finger" of the VIP strip and stick it on the word. Let them know that they don't actually have to read the text to do this.

3. When time is up, bring students together. Ask for volunteers from each group to come forward to share one word the group found and to explain how they found it. Was it written in a different color from the rest of the text? Was it underlined or in italics? Was one kind of word easier to notice than another?

4. In a concluding discussion, be sure students understand that a) not all important words in a text are treated this way; but b) all words treated this way *are* important. Be sure, too, that students realize the connection between highlighted words and glossaries.

INFORMATIONAL TEXT—BIG PRINT, BIG IDEAS

Explanation

This lesson helps students notice the obvious—the headings and subheadings on a text page. In a unique way, students learn to—literally—call attention to big, bold print.

Skill Focus

Using text features/organizers to obtain information; identifying parts of a book; identifying characteristics of genres; categorizing and classifying words and ideas

Materials & Resources

Text

- Any grade-appropriate informational text with headings and subheadings (a Big Book would be ideal)

Other

- Pointer

Bonus Ideas

Find a page of informational text that has strong features—headings, subheadings, diagrams, captions, and so on. Make photocopies and then cut each apart into pieces, keeping the features intact. Bundle each set with paper clips and pass out to students. Their job is to reconstruct the page, using as a guideline the appropriate and/or probable positions for the features.

STEPS

1. Tell students that the size of print on a page can provide a clue to its importance. Another clue is how dark the print looks. When authors have a big idea that they want to share, they call attention to it by making it larger and darker. You might say something like, "You could think about it as the author using a louder voice with certain important words in the book. The author wants to be sure we 'hear' the big print."

2. Gather students together and display a page of print that includes headings and subheadings. Ask the class if they notice anything about the size of the print on the page. Allow students to come up and use your pointer to indicate the larger type.

3. Tell students that you're all going to read the page together. You want them to do something special when you come to the larger, darker print. You want them to make a "megaphone" with their hands. Demonstrate how to do this by cupping your hands around your mouth. Discuss briefly what a megaphone is, how it looks, and how it's used—to amplify someone's voice.

4. Now explain to students that before they actually get to use their hand megaphones, they need to understand how to do this inside a building. Naturally, they can't use truly loud voices. So, when they use their "megaphones," they are going to pretend to yell. Teach them to yell with only a whisper voice. (If some students are unsure what a "whisper voice" is, have them practice by putting their fingers on their throat: they should notice a difference in how their voice box feels when talk and when they whisper.)

5. After students have practiced their special indoor megaphone voices, invite them to read the page aloud with you. Each time you come to a heading or subheading, you should all cup your hands and speak those words through the "megaphones."

6. Have students use assigned or independent informational reading books to practice this activity with partners. Conclude the lesson by reviewing the rationale behind using the megaphone voices: the larger, darker words—the "big" words—are also the big ideas in the text.

Seeing the Structure of Sequence

Explanation

Unlike the other lessons in this section (which focus on external text signals), this lesson examines a common internal text structure. Students are asked to work with three key sequence words as they reinforce their understanding of time order in text.

Skill Focus

Using text features/organizers to obtain information; identifying characteristics of genres; categorizing and classifying words and ideas

Materials & Resources

Text

- A narrative text with simple sequence (Used in this lesson: "The Lion and the Mouse" from *The Lion & the Mouse and Other Aesop's Fables* retold by Doris Orgel)

Other

- Sentence strips
- Multiple index cards: one with the word *first*, several with the word *next*, and one with the word *last* (Note: You'll need as many *next* cards as there are major events in the story)
- Pocket chart

Steps

1. Review the concept of sequence. Remind students that in informational text facts are often presented in first-next-last order, such as the chain of events that seeds follow to become corn (lesson on page 69). Remind students, too, that the events in stories follow a pattern—they always have a beginning, middle, and end (lessons on pages 92–94).
2. Display the index cards. Point out that this time structure is so important because it helps stories to make sense. So today students will have another chance to work with sequence and with the three important time words: *first, next, last.*
3. Tell students that the sequence of what happened first, next, and last is important in today's story. You want them to listen carefully to what happens in the story so that they can help you remember what happened first, next, and last.
4. Read aloud the model book.
5. Post the blank sentence strips. Write the story title on one strip. Then invite students to help you recall the events of the story. On the remaining strips write complete sentences that describe these events—one event per strip.
6. Call attention to the pocket chart. Place the strips in the chart, with the title at the top and then all events in order from first to last. Read aloud the events and, as you do so, place the appropriate index card parallel to that event. An example chart and set of cards for the sample book are on page 112 at the end of this lesson.
7. Remove the strips and distribute them to partner groups or groups of three—one to each group. Have students discuss briefly where their event occurs in the story—first, next (in the middle), or last.
8. Challenge students to reconstruct the story. Read aloud each index card and have groups bring their strips to the pocket chart at the appropriate time.
9. With the class, read through the strips again. Have students determine if the story makes sense.

Bonus Ideas

To create a literacy center activity that allows students to practice sequencing independently, package folded sentence strips and index cards from this lesson's story (as well as from additional familiar stories) in a large snap or seal bag. Set up a pocket chart in the center. Have students reconstruct the stories by appropriately positioning the sentence strips and the index cards.

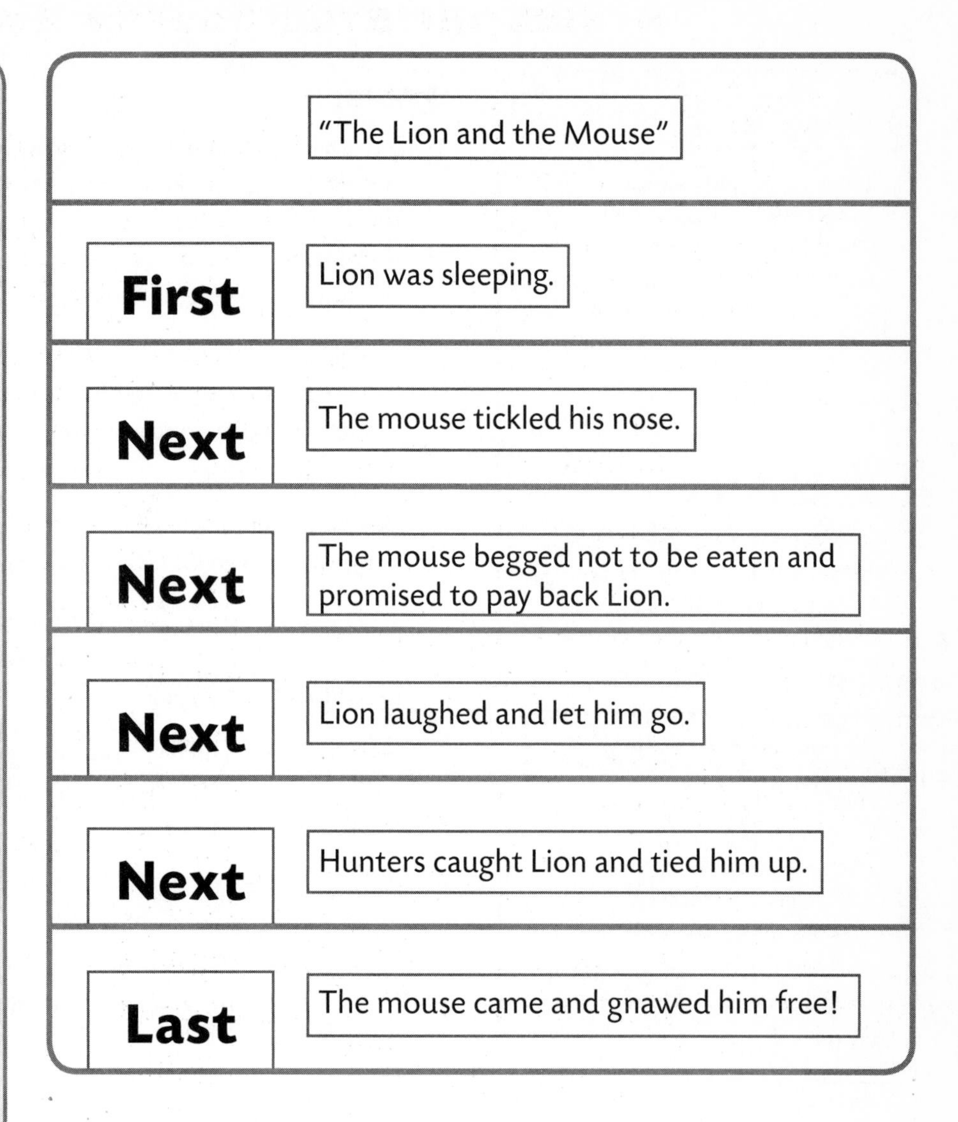

GETTING STARTED WITH POETRY

Explanation

Children quickly develop a love for poetry. It's important to expose them to lots and lots of poetry to help develop their phonemic awareness and to allow them to play with language. This lesson calls attention to how poetry differs from prose.

Skill Focus

Using text features/organizers to obtain information; identifying characteristics of genres; categorizing and classifying words and ideas; recognizing rhythm, rhyme, and patterned structures in poetry

Materials & Resources

Text

- A poem and a brief story based on the same topic (Used in this lesson: "The Firefly" in *Beast Feast* by Douglas Florian and *The Very Lonely Firefly* by Eric Carle)

Bonus Ideas

Using large type, type up and print out a poem of five to ten lines. Make several photocopies. For each copy, cut apart the lines and place them in an envelope. Have small groups or partners experiment with the lines, laying them out in different ways, to find the order they like best that makes sense.

STEPS

1. Tell students that in today's lesson they will have a chance to experience the same subject in two ways. They will hear a poem and a story about the same topic. They'll need to be paying careful attention and thinking the whole time because afterward you're going to ask them to point out similarities and differences between the two kinds of texts.

2. Read the poem and the story to or with students. As you read, hold up both texts so that students can see the text on the page. After reading, leave both books propped open to provide visual reminders of how the texts look.

3. Draw a Venn diagram on the board. Above one circle, write the name of the poem, and above the other, the name of the story.

4. Invite students to tell you how the two texts are alike and how they're different. List the differences in the discrete parts of the Venn circles. List the likenesses in the circles' combined portion. For example, a Venn diagram for the sample texts might look like this:

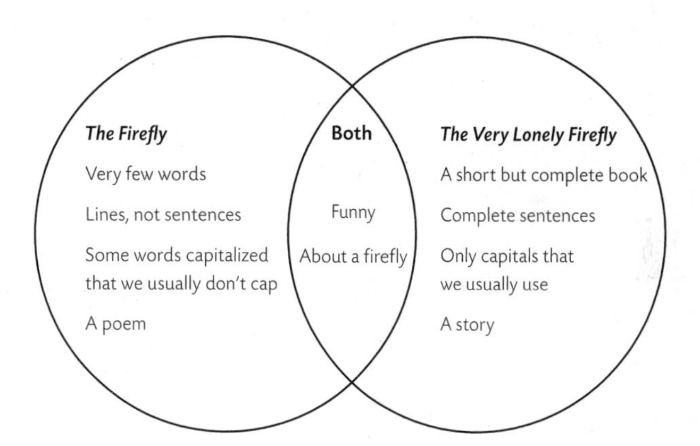

5. After students have pointed out these likenesses and differences, engage them in a class discussion about the unique characteristics of poems. Characteristics you might note follow:

   - It often uses rhyming words.
   - It doesn't have to be written in complete sentences.
   - Sometimes the sentences or lines are arranged the way we normally talk.
   - The words can be spaced oddly. Sometimes they create shapes.
   - Poems use fewer words to tell about things.
   - Poems don't use the same rules for writing that we usually use.

6. Be sure to have many poetry books available so that students can explore this fun genre whenever they have free time!

GETTING STARTED WITH DRAMA

Explanation

First graders have a natural talent for acting. As in two related lessons (pages 78 and 91), you'll find that they love to dramatize anything and everything. More challenging than the earlier lessons, this one engages students in creating a drama from an informational text while teaching them, at the same time, about basic drama conventions and formatting. The resulting dialogue will be simple, but your students will love this activity! And, the added benefit is...you'll get to see what they've comprehended from the text.

Skill Focus

Using text features/organizers to obtain information; identifying characteristics of genres, including drama; categorizing and classifying words and ideas; reading aloud fluently (with appropriate pacing, phrasing, intonation, rhythm)

Materials & Resources

Text

- A grade-appropriate informational text that lends itself to the development of characters (Used in this lesson: *Bugs! Bugs! Bugs!* By Jennifer Dussling)
- Plays and drama anthologies, such as *Show Time: Music, Dance, and Drama Activities for Kids* by Lisa Bany-Winters or *101 Drama Games for Children: Fun and Learning with Acting and Make-Believe* by Paul Rooyackers and Cecilia Bowman

Note that although we have not broken this lesson into two parts, the lesson will need to span several days, especially if you incorporate a performance.

Prior to the Lesson: *For a week or two before this lesson, make available to students grade-appropriate plays and drama anthologies (see Materials & Resources). You might create a special display of these books in your classroom library and set up dedicated time for students to read through the books, in pairs or in small groups.*

STEPS

1. Tell students that today they are going to get a chance to put to use their growing knowledge of drama and plays. Call attention to key characteristics and conventions of the plays students have been browsing through. These include:
    - Directions for the actors, enclosed in parentheses. Be sure students realize that the parts in parentheses aren't read aloud. They are only to tell the actors what to do.
    - A character's name listed when it is his or her turn to speak.
    - Colons (:), not quotation marks, to show that someone is talking.
2. Read aloud your selected text. Tell students that you want to work with them to write a drama about something you've all learned from this book. For example, for the sample book, you might say, "Caterpillars can't talk, but let's write a drama or play as if caterpillars can tell us about themselves. First we'll need to summarize the facts we've learned about these bugs. Then we'll need to remember all our knowledge about how plays are written. And when we're done, we can perform our play!"
3. List key facts that students have learned about caterpillars. Here is one sample list:
    - Caterpillars have long hairs that break easily.
    - Their enemies sometimes get a mouthful of these hairs!
    - Sometimes they huddle together to be safe.
    - They spin cocoons and live in a chrysalis while they change.
    - They turn into beautiful butterflies.
    - Their bright colors mean that they might taste bad to their enemies.

Other

- Chart paper
- Multiple photocopies of the play that the class writes

Bonus Ideas

An easy but beautiful backdrop can be created in minutes! Use a transparency as your canvas. Draw your scenery, leaving blank the middle portion, where the actors will stand. Choose a suitable classroom wall and pull your overhead projector back so that you can project onto the wall. Line up the bottom of the transparency where the wall and floor meet, covering as much of the wall as you wish. Voila! You now have a terrific backdrop for your play.

4. Now work with students to transform these facts into a drama. To get started, ask how many parts they feel they need. Continue by asking leading questions, such as:
   - Should all our characters be caterpillars?
   - What could our characters say and do to let our audience know about facts we've learned?
   - What directions can we add that will help our actors do a better job?
   - What end punctuation will help our actors know how to say their lines?

5. Here is one example of a drama based on the facts about caterpillars:

Drama based on *Bugs! Bugs! Bugs!*

All Caterpillars (*crawl and nibble*): We are caterpillars. We crawl and eat all day!

Caterpillar 1: I have long hair.

Bug 1 (*makes a face!*): I tried to eat him and got a mouth full of hair!

All Caterpillars (*joining together*): Sometimes we huddle together. It makes us look scary!

Caterpillar 2 (*goes around and around*): I'm spinning a cocoon of silk.

Caterpillar 3 (*pretends to knock*): Now there's a hard chrysalis around him.

Caterpillars 4 and 5 (*lift up their hands*): Shhhhh! He's sleeping!

Caterpillar 6: I think he's about to wake up!

All Caterpillars: Look! (*point*) He's a beautiful butterfly now!

Bug 2: I know to stay away from those bright colors. They don't taste good!

All Caterpillars: We'll become butterflies, too, one day!

Caterpillar 7 (*clasps hands together*): I can't wait to fly!

6. Once you have created your script, it's time to perform your drama. Assign parts and allow students to practice reading their parts until they're fluent. Then enjoy your production!

A Keyboard Print

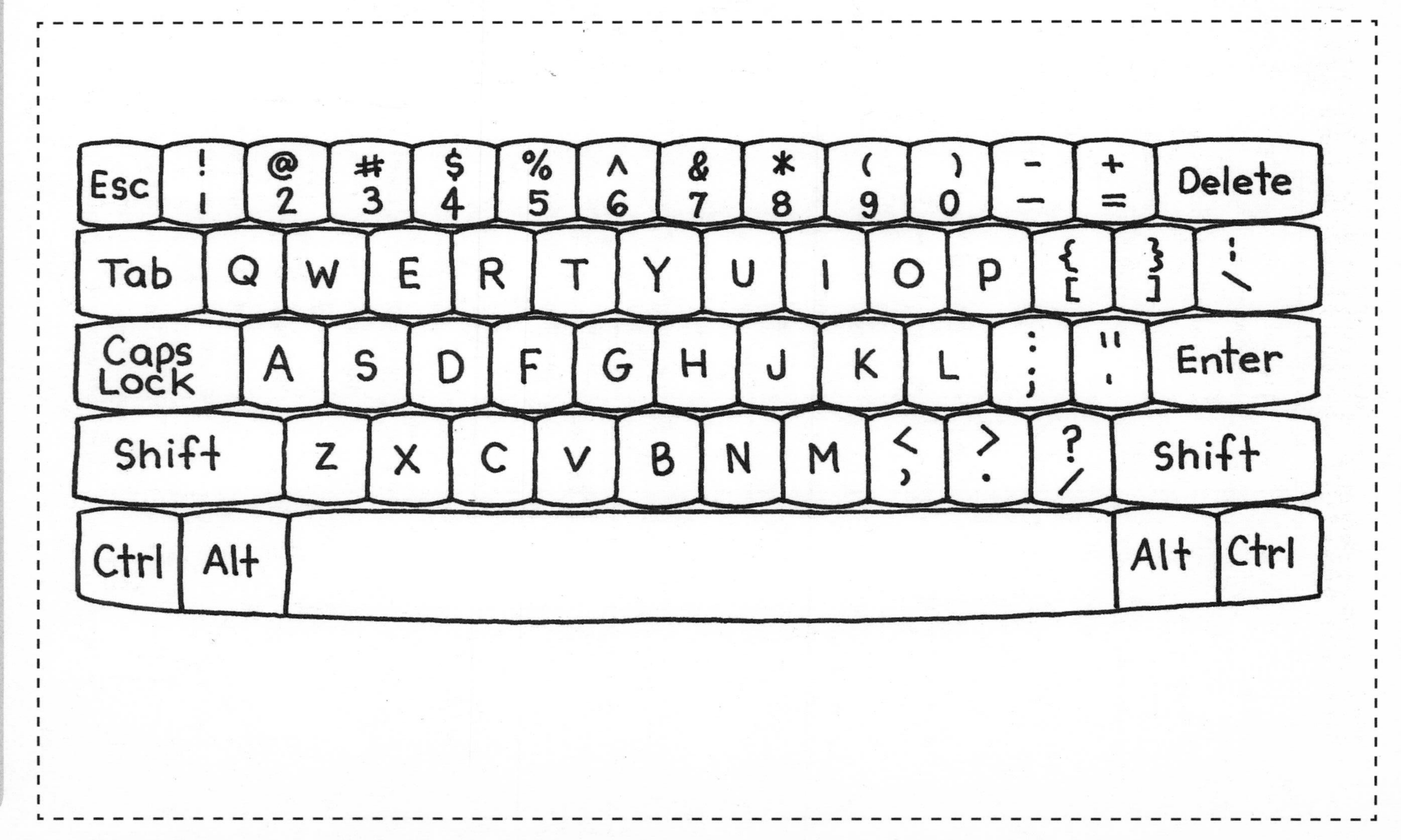

Character Outlines Organizer

Story Hand Buttons

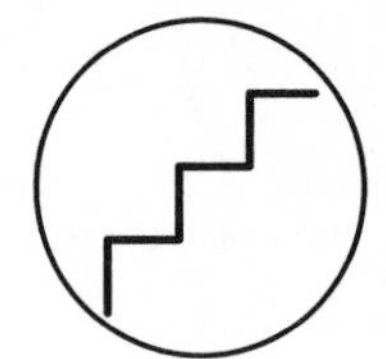

Eyeglass Frame

Comparing Story Elements Chart

	Story:	Story:
Characters		
Setting		
Plot		
Problem		
Solution		
Kind of Story		

Cyclical Map Cut-Outs

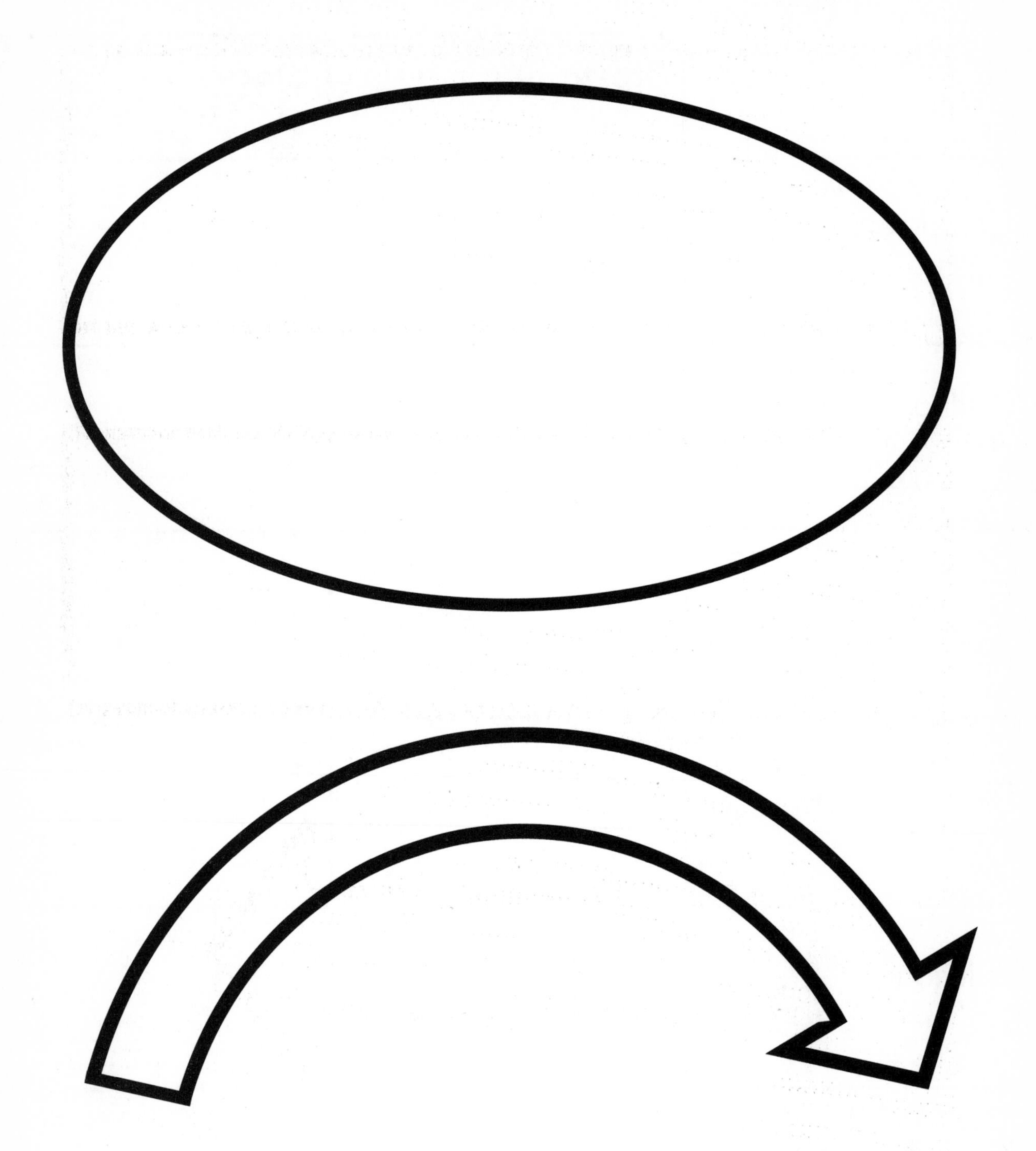

Sequential Map Cut-Outs

Artist's Storyboard

Here's the main character . . .	First . . .	Here's an event . . .	Here's an event . . .
Here's an event . . .	And another event . . .	And another event . . .	Here's what happens at the end . . .

Name: ______________________ Word: ______________

Know Your Words

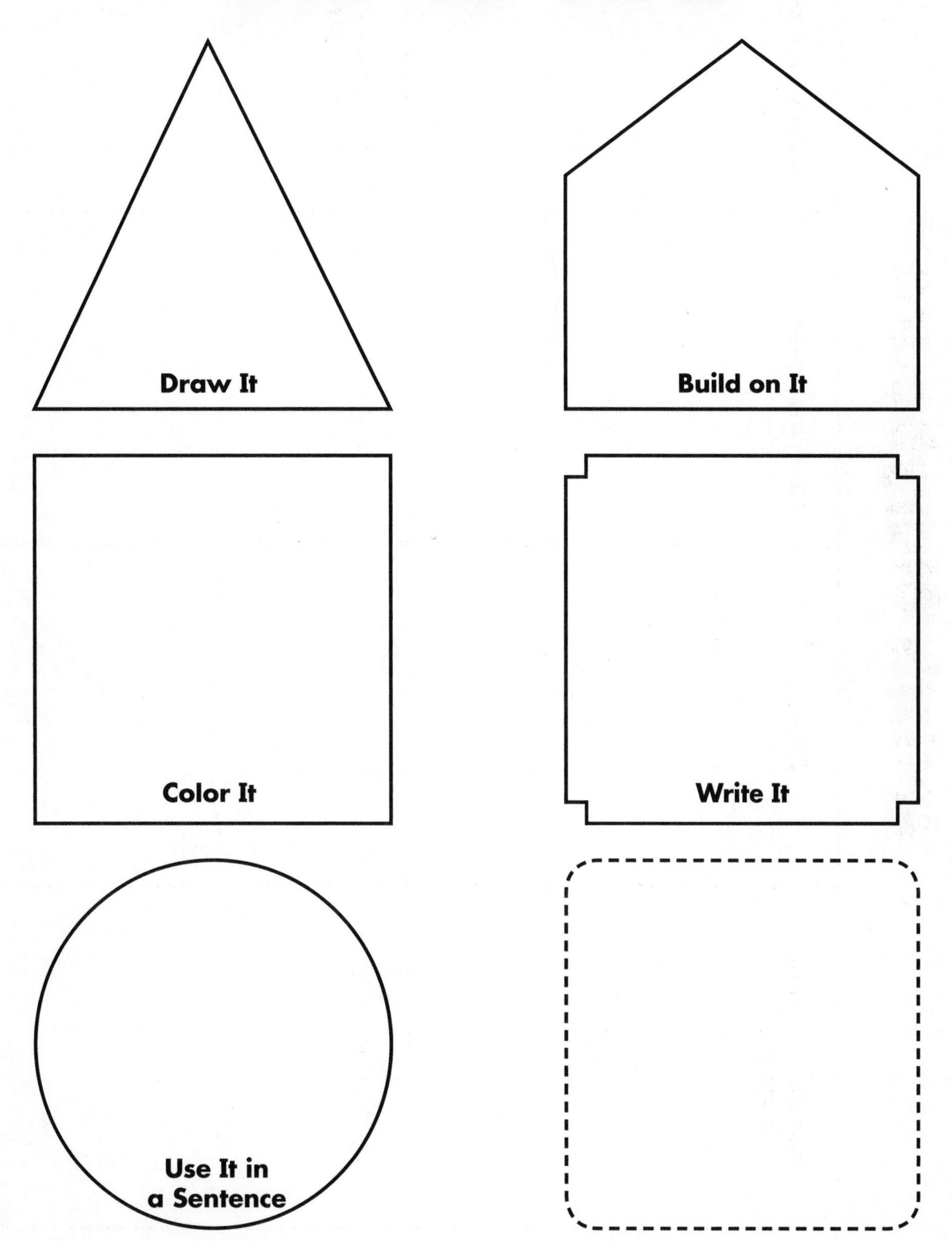

Bee Outline

Name: ______________________ **Date:** ______________________

Informational Text Chart

Topic: ____

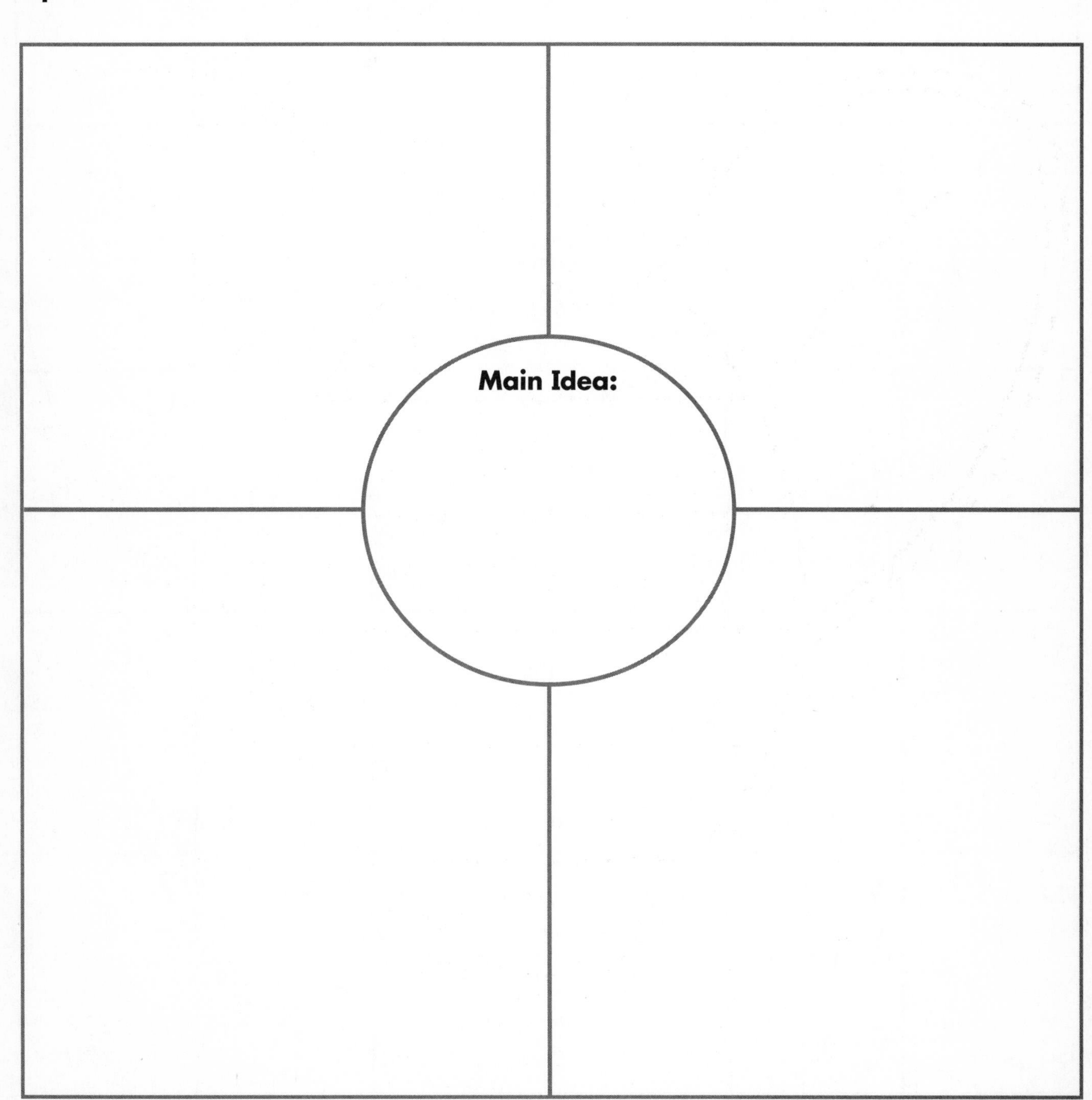

Alpha-Key Words Chart

A	B	C	D	E	F
G	H	**Topic**		I	J
K	L			M	N
O	P	Q	R	S	T
U	V	W	X	Y	Z

Bibliography

Asch, F. (1997). *Moonbear's pet.* New York: Simon & Schuster Books for Young Readers.

Bany-winters, L. (2000). *Show time: Music, dance, and drama activities for kids.* Chicago, IL: Chicago Review Press.

Borduin, B. J., Borduin, C. M., & Manley, C. M. (1994). The use of imagery training to improve reading comprehension of second graders. *The Journal of Genetic Psychology, 155*(1), 115–118.

Bromley, K., Irwin-De Vitis, L., & Modlo, M. (1995). *Graphic organizers: Visual strategies for active learning.* New York: Scholastic.

Bunting, E. (1997). *Ducky.* New York: Clarion Books.

Bunting, E. (1994). *Flower garden.* San Diego, CA: Harcourt Trade Publishers.

Bunting, E. (1991). *Fly away home.* New York: Clarion Books.

Bunting, E. (2004). *My special day at third street school.* Honesdale, PA: Boyds Mills Press.

Carle, E. (1995). *The very lonely firefly.* New York: Philomel Books.

Carmack, L. J. (1998). *Philippe in Monet's garden.* Boston, MA: Museum of Fine Arts.

Christelow, E. (1989). *Five little monkeys.* New York: Clarion Books.

Collins, R. (2004). *Flies for dinner.* DeSoto, TX: McGraw-Hill Wright Group.

Curtis, J. L. (1998). *Today I feel silly & other moods that make my day.* New York: Joanna Cotler/HarperCollins Publishers.

Curtis, J. L. (1993). *When I was little: A four-year-old's memoir of her youth.* Joanna Cotler/HarperCollins Publishers.

Curtis, J. L. (2000). *Where do balloons go? An uplifting mystery.* Joanna Cotler/HarperCollins Publishers

dePaola, T. (1977). *The quicksand book.* New York: Holiday House.

Dole, J.A., Duffy, G.G., Roehler, L.R. & Pearson, P.D. (1991). Moving from the old to the new: Research on reading comprehension instruction. *Review of Educational Research,* (61), 239-264.

Durkin, D. (1993). *Teaching them to read* (6th ed.). Boston, MA: Allyn & Bacon.

Dussling, J. (1998). *Bugs! bugs! bugs!* New York: Dorling Kindersley Publishing.

Ehlert, L. (1987). *Growing vegetable soup.* New York: Harcourt Children's Books.

Florian, D. (1994). The firefly. In *Beast feast: poems.* San Diego, CA: Harcourt Trade Publishers.

Fowler, A. (1999). *Our living forests.* New York: Children's Press.

Gambrell, L. B. & Koskinen, P. S. (2002). Imagery: A strategy for enhancing comprehension. In C. C. Block & M. Pressley (Eds.), *Comprehension instruction: Research-based best practices* (pp. 305–318). New York: Guilford Press.

Garland, M. (2003). *Miss Smith's incredible storybook.* New York: Dutton Juvenile.

Gibbons, G. (1997). *The moon book.* New York: Holiday House.

Gibbons, G. (1993). *Spiders.* New York: Holiday House.

Griffiths, R., & Clyne, M. (2004). *Animal look-alikes.* Parsippany, NJ: Pearson Learning Group.

Halpern, J. (1998). *A look at spiders.* Austin, TX: Raintree Steck-Vaughn Publishers.

Harris, T. L., & Hodges, R. E. (1995). *The literacy dictionary: The vocabulary of reading and writing.* Newark, DE: International Reading Association.

BIBLIOGRAPHY

Hayden, K. (2003). *Amazing buildings*. New York: Dorling Kindersley Publishing.

Henkes, K. (2004). *Kitten's first full moon*. New York: Greenwillow Books.

Henkes, K. (1996). *Lilly's purple plastic purse*. New York: Greenwillow Books.

Henkes, K. (1993). *Owen*. New York: Greenwillow Books.

Hoyt, L. (1999). *Revisit, reflect, retell: Strategies for improving reading comprehension*. Portsmouth, NH: Heinemann.

Keene, E. O., & Zimmermann, S. (1997). *Mosaic of thought: Teaching comprehension in a reader's workshop*. Portsmouth, NH: Heinemann.

Kellogg, S. (1977). *The mysterious tadpole*. New York: The Dial Press.

Levin, J. R., & Divine-Hawkins, P. (1974). Visual imagery as a prose-learning process. *Journal of Reading Behavior*, (6), 23–30.

Manning, M., & Granstrom, B. (1998). *Splish, splash, splosh!* New York: Franklin Watts.

Mead, K. (1998). *How spiders got eight legs*. Austin, TX: Raintree Steck-Vaughn Publishers.

National Reading Panel Report (2000). Bethesda, MD: National Reading Panel.

Nayer, J. (1996). *Pancakes!* Parsippany, NJ: Modern Curriculum Press.

Numeroff, L. J. (1985). *If You Give a Mouse a Cookie*. New York: Laura Geringer/HarperCollins Publishers.

Orgel, D. (retold) (2000). The lion and the mouse. In *The lion & the mouse and other Aesop fables*. New York: Dorling Kindersley Publishing.

Pearson, P.D & Duke, N. K. (2002). Chapter 10: Effective practices for developing reading comprehension. In *What research has to say about reading instruction* (3rd ed.). Newark, DE: International Reading Association.

Pinkwater, D. (1999). *The Hoboken chicken emergency*. New York: Aladdin.

Robson, P. (1998). *What's for lunch? Corn*. New York: Children's Press.

Rooyackers, P. & Bowman, C. (1997). *101 drama games for children: fun and learning with acting and make-believe*. Alameda, CA: Hunter House Publishers.

Rosenberg, E. (1995). *May I go out?* Parsippany, NJ: Modern Curriculum Press.

Sigmon, C. M., & Ford, S. M. (2005). *Writing lessons for the content areas*. New York: Scholastic.

Siomades, L. (1999). *The itsy bitsy spider*. Honesdale, PA: Boyds Mills Press.

Thompson, G. (1997). *Bear facts*. Austin, TX: Raintree Steck-Vaughn Publishers.

Tovani, C. (2000). *I read it, but I don't get it!* Denver, CO: Stenhouse Publishers.

Wallace, K. (2001). *Rockets and spaceships*. New York: Dorling Kindersley Publishing.

Willis, S. (1999). *Tell me why rain is wet (whiz kids)*. London, England: Franklin Watts.

Warner, G. C. (1990). *The boxcar children: the yellow house mystery*. Niles, IL: Albert Whitman & Company.

Wood, A. (1982). *Quick as a cricket*. Swindon, England: Child's Play (International) Ltd.

Wood, D. (1998). *Making the world*. New York: Simon & Schuster Books for Young Readers.

www.enchantedlearning.com